Every Pilgrim's Guide to Walking to Santiago de Compostela

Peter Müller
and
Angel Fernández de Aránguiz SCA

Translated from the Spanish by
Laurie Dennett

CANTERBURY
PRESS
Norwich

© Peter Müller and Angel Fernández de Aránguiz SCA 2010

Translated by Laurie Dennett

This edition published in 2010 by
the Canterbury Press Norwich
Editorial office
13–17 Long Lane,
London, EC1A 9PN, UK

Canterbury Press is an imprint of Hymns Ancient and
Modern Ltd (a registered charity)
13A Hellesdon Park Road, Norwich,
Norfolk, NR6 5DR, UK

www.scm-canterburypress.co.uk

First published in Germany as *Wer aufbricht, kommt
auch heim* in 1993 (second edition 2009), by Verlag am
Eschbach der Schwabenverlag AG (and in Spanish as
El Camino Lleva a Casa in 2004).

Bible extracts are from the Authorized Version of the Bible
(The King James Bible), the rights in which are vested in
the Crown, are reproduced by permission of the Crown's
Patentee, Cambridge University Press.

British Library Cataloguing in Publication data
A catalogue record for this book is available
from the British Library

978 1 84825 026 0

Typeset by Regent Typesetting, London
Printed and bound in Great Britain by
CPI Bookmarque, Croydon CRO 4TD

Contents

The restless heart is the starting point of pilgrimage. Everyone harbours a longing that impels him or her to leave behind the indifference of everyday life and the narrowness of habitual surroundings. Things that are different and strange always attract. None the less, the novelty a person sees and experiences along the way can never completely fill this longing. The longing is greater. In the depths of the heart, each person is constantly seeking the fullest identification with the Other. All the paths along which humankind advances point to the fact that life is a path, a way of pilgrimage towards God.

St Augustine

An anonymous poem on a wall outside Nájera

Dust, mud, thirst and rain
Is the Way of St James,
Thousands of pilgrims
And more than a thousand years.

Pilgrim, who summons you?
What secret power draws you?
Not the field of the stars,
Nor the vast cathedrals,

Not the historic valour of Navarre,
Nor the wine of La Rioja,
Nor Galicia's feasts of shellfish,
Nor the fields of Castile.

Pilgrim, who summons you?
What hidden force attracts you?
Not the people along the way,
Nor the rural hospitality.

It's not history and culture,
Or the miracle of La Calzada,
Not the palace of Gaudí,
Or the castle of Ponferrada.

I see it all as I pass by,
And it's a joy to see it all,
But the voice that summons me
I feel in my very depths.

The force that impels me,
The power that draws me
I can't quite explain.
Only the Almighty can do that!

translated by Laurie Dennett

Translated with the encouragement of,
and in memory of,
D. Angel Fernández SCA
(2 October 1942 – 13 June 2009)

Pilgrim, remember him especially at the albergues of
Azofra, Santibáñez de Valdeiglesias, Hospital de Orbigo,
Foncebadón, El Acebo, Ponferrada and La Faba, all of which
he guided into existence without ever seeking thanks or
recognition, in the true spirit of the *Camino*.

Invitation

Santiago de Compostela, the capital of Galicia in the north-west of the Iberian peninsula, is the city of the Apostle St James the Great, the patron saint of Spain. Many people travel to Santiago nowadays, and always end up going back. What is it about this city that captures their interest? Is it a place of pilgrimage where one visits the tomb of an Apostle or the historic and artistic focal point of an ancient and important cultural phenomenon? Do the visitors come to venerate the Apostle who accompanied Jesus in his public ministry or to fulfil a vow? Do they bring to it something desired or hoped for? Perhaps Santiago is only an encouragement to break the monotony of everyday life or to let curiosity reign, to imagine oneself in different circumstances, getting to know other people, surroundings or geographical features.

From the time of the discovery of the Apostle's tomb early in the ninth century, through the era when the pilgrimage was at its height, up to today, when the past 30 years have again brought about enormous interest in this European pilgrimage route, we find the most varied of motives, expressed in different modes of travel according to the underlying objective. Not all motivations are in keeping with the spirit, meaning and aim of the Way of St James. Some are open to human and religious experience, others make this difficult or even prevent it. None the less these all belong to any journey along the Way, given that if it were otherwise, its meaning – and with it an essential treasure-house of experience – would remain inaccessible. The following anecdote illustrates this:

A globetrotter arrived in Santiago to pay his respects to the Apostle and pray at his tomb. Neither in the cathedral nor kneeling before the reliquary did he succeed in pulling his thoughts together. His lips formed empty phrases and his mind was elsewhere. After various fruitless attempts, he came across two men sitting in silence in the cathedral. They looked like pilgrims, and he asked their advice. 'How long have you been here?' one of them asked him. 'Since yesterday. I came by plane', the traveller replied. 'Well, be patient. Your spirit will arrive a bit later. It needs more time. It's still making its way here, as this journey is usually done on foot. The point is, the Way is also the destination.'

The Way is the destination. For such a destination, time is needed: to go across country, to follow every twist and turn, you have to give yourself over to it, immerse yourself in it completely – body, soul and spirit. This refines your perception of how it has evolved historically and in the present day, the diversity of art forms and their message, culture in all its manifestations, the changing landscapes, the people who live along the *Camino de Santiago*. This openness facilitates personal experience and the guidance of those who are searching. You experience, in a new way, that the pilgrimage route to Santiago de Compostela is, on the one hand, a concrete reality with many dimensions of experience and, on the other, a symbol of that state of being 'on the way' proper to human existence – or rather, in the words of Don Julián Barrio Barrio, Archbishop of Santiago, 'a metaphor for life'.

For the medieval pilgrim, the pilgrimage along the *Camino* was an image, a living experience that bore him along and oriented his earthly life until his meeting with Christ, the righteous judge, and eternal rest in God. A modern German song conveys this idea:

Only guests on earth	*Wir sind nur Gast auf Erden*
We wander without rest	*und wandern ohne Ruh*
With ceaseless weariness	*mit mancherlei Beschwerden*
Towards the eternal	*der ewigen Heimat zu.*
homeland.	

The true pilgrimage way was, and is, life itself. This approach is also consistent with the Christian view of life. Being 'on the way' includes, and gives a name to, a fundamental situation of human existence. The chapter 'Setting the Scene' introduces the metaphor of 'the way', and the religious understanding of it and of the pilgrimage to Santiago in general.

This book is not just another guidebook to the Way of St James (in Spanish, *el Camino de Santiago*). Properly speaking it is a spiritual *vademecum*: that is, a companion that aims to help us to see more. It seeks to focus on the spiritual approach to the symbols of being 'on the way' and of the Way of St James, on the appreciation and interpretation of selected works of art and cultural monuments, as well as on the meaning of the pilgrimage.

The idea of writing it arose during many trips and journeys with individuals and groups undertaking the Spanish section of the Way of St James. The experience of travelling the route on an individual or collective basis – whether on foot, alone or accompanied, or on organized tours, walking specific stretches – caused certain topics to come together as material and subjects for explanation and study. Many people's interest in reading and reflecting about them, not only while on the Camino, but also at home, was an encouragement to give them shape and form.

This little book, in its simplicity and provision of information to help you see and interpret, aims to open – and bring you closer to – the religious, human and historical dimension of the Way of St James, inviting reflection and possible interior growth. It can be used equally well by tourists and pilgrims, and by each according to his or her chosen mode of travel.

The basic mode of making a pilgrimage is on foot. Ever more people are doing part or parts of the Camino. Being continually on the move physically is an aid to spiritual agility. Movement loosens the muscles and we become more aware of ourselves and of others, of our surroundings and of nature, of our brothers and sisters, and finally of God. One begins to change inwardly (in theological terms, we speak of conversion). Someone may set off, already a pilgrim; none the less, whoever sets off exposes herself or himself to change, and changes. A pilgrim is *made*. This book should be of particular use to pilgrims who are walking. Its layout, in parts organized around themes, stretches of the Way and material for reflection, allows each person to select what at any particular point is most convenient.

Because of its practicality and organization, this book may be best used on a preliminary journey, getting to know and reflecting upon the Way of St James, which may include walking certain stretches. Many people are unable to carry a rucksack because of age, health or other reasons. They can still understand and benefit from the spirit of the pilgrimage. The key to understanding the Way of St James lies in the spirit of the pilgrimage. The concept of *peregrinatio* – of what it is to make a pilgrimage – is therefore what determines the spiritual dimension, together with the way the journey or study trip is made. This was already being asserted in the sixteenth century. Hieronymus Turler, the author of a treatise on travel published in 1574 under the title *De peregrinatione*, describes travelling (in contrast to the pleasant pastime of being a wanderer or vagabond) as 'an activity through which to learn to know other lands for one's own benefit and that of one's country'. In this sense, then and now, travellers and pilgrims meet on the Way of St James; not surprisingly, it has been declared the 'First European Cultural Itinerary'. They wish to come together in peace with people from the other countries of Europe and of the world. But in addition, in the words of Pope John Paul II, in a homily given on 10 August 1980:

> to go on pilgrimage is to go beyond the horizon of visible things to the invisible reality of God. Roads, pathways, motorways, bridges, landscapes, castles, cemeteries, churches, monuments, villages, cities, men, women, furnishings ... everything has to contribute to our genuine understanding of the pilgrim nature of humankind.

Many people, for different reasons, have not been able to or can no longer experience the Way of St James directly. This book can help them to understand and relive something of what in times past and for centuries, it meant to our ancestors to make the pilgrimage. Understanding their experience, we may better understand our own, however critical the latter may be. Generally speaking the point is better understood when one has travelled the *Camino*; one has a broader vision. The *Camino* permits us to grasp its meaning. The paramount importance of the *Camino* was such that the *Liber Sancti Jacobi* (described on p. xxi) portrayed it as, in a sense, even more important than the end of the journey: we owe the saying 'the pilgrimage road leads men to life' to this conviction.

Finally, a small point: in Spain it is often thought that because the country has more or less a common history, and because Santiago de Compostela is situated there and an essential portion of the *Camino de Santiago* is there, everything of any significance is to be found in a Spanish context. But the Way was not created only by Spanish pilgrims, rather by all those who travelled it, many of whom were – as they continue to be – from elsewhere. There is no *Camino* without pilgrims, and in this book there can also be read something of what pilgrims have written about it. In the adaptation of this book for English-speaking readers, we have included, with the permission of their creators, poems, extracts, reflections and photographs by English-speaking pilgrims. It is hoped that the existence of such material, as well as of the rich heritage of devotion to St James and the pilgrimage in the British Isles, may add to readers' interest and knowledge.

Our desire is that this book be a companion on the Way, and that on the route, readers and those directly involved may experience that Compostela is the goal, the *Camino* is 'the way' and that the liberation and the inward experiences of faith – all together – are the energy for the pilgrimage of life.

Ultreia et suseia! Deus adjuvat nos!
Onward and forward! May God be with us!

Setting the Scene

Year after year people set off along the Way of St James: on vacation, to see new places, to leave everyday life behind and relax, to meet other people. Some go on study tours, to see towns and cities, the art and culture of their own and other countries. Others go on pilgrimage for religious reasons. Finally, not a few take themselves off to the silence of a monastery, to calm reflection, in search of self-awareness. They all have in common a certain longing that aspires to external changes and internal transformations. With the desire for 'a breath of fresh air' there arises in many people the longing to concentrate their attention on the search for something more than the material and physical realities of every day.

That longing prompts many people to set out along the *Camino de Santiago* to Compostela. They want to see the monasteries, towns and cities along it. They enjoy visiting the museums and churches, and getting to know the customs and the history. But they are looking for something more than these. They are seekers of the significance and meaning of the Way of St James, and of a 'way' for themselves, and perhaps for others besides themselves. They are on a search, 'on the way', like the two monks in the following Russian legend:

There were two monks who, together, read in an old book that the end of the world was to be found where the sky and the earth met. They decided to go and search for it and not to return until they had found it. They wandered the world, faced countless dangers, suffered all kinds of hardships – everything that wandering through the world might involve and every temptation that might cause someone to abandon the determined goal. They had read that there existed a door, at which it was only necessary to knock, and one would be face to face with God. At last they found what they were looking for. Trembling, they knocked at the door and watched it open. Once they were inside they suddenly realized that they were in a cell of their own monastery. They then understood that the place where the sky and the earth meet is to be found in this world, in the place that God has assigned to us.

The longing of both monks was awakened by reading 'an old book'. In a similar fashion, in the Middle Ages the desire to go to Santiago de Compostela was spread by pilgrim stories, accounts and songs, and above all by the pilgrims' guide that was part of the twelfth-century *Codex Calixtinus*. Who hasn't had this experience? A novel or a story, something mentioned or a person, a specific word or a piece of news, an illness or a meeting has an impact that moves me to ponder about myself and what I desire. The longing of those monks on their search takes shape at the moment they set off on their journey. They feel it in body and soul while they are on the move, and they experience it on arrival. They enter their own monastic cell and understand that they, as seekers, are always 'on the way' – not just anywhere, but in the life they lead. That is the place 'where the sky and the earth meet'. Life is a 'road' or 'pathway', and I am on it as a pilgrim, searching. But what exactly does that mean?

Life as Pilgrimage

The word *Camino*, or way, road, path, implies movement. I am continually in movement in time and space; externally and internally I am 'on the road' or way. Using the image of the road, human existence can be easily described or interpreted.

The road or way is a venerable symbol that we find in many religions. The early Christians used it, including self-referentially, and called themselves 'followers of the (new) way'. For this reason, making a pilgrimage along the Way of St James is for many Christians a possible means and way of expressing the condition of being 'on the way', to experience it spiritually and psychically, and to work out the interpretations of their own life-paths.

The Way, as a metaphor for our lives, takes in everything: what moves us and what tires us, the person who encounters us and the things that happen to us, what we discern and what we put up with, what we aspire to and what we achieve, what we make our own and what we let go, what we tolerate and what we change. The physical reality of being 'on the way' and its psycho-spiritual feeling are two faces of an experience of wholeness. In body and soul, as whole people, we set out along 'the way'.

The *Codex Calixtinus*

The *Codex Calixtinus*, a manuscript compiled some time between 1160 and 1170, is also known as the *Liber Sancti Jacobi*, or Book of St James, and consists of five books. The first four were, it seems, brought together by Aymeric Picaud, a monk from Parthenay-le-Vieux in France, who himself then wrote the fifth. These five books contain:

- Readings, sermons, liturgical and other texts for the feast days and celebrations in honour of the Apostle St James.
- A narrative of 22 miracles attributed to St James.
- An account of the translation of the mortal remains of St James to Galicia.
- The so-called *Pseudo-Turpin*: an account of Charlemagne's campaign in Spain.
- The *Pilgrim's Guide*; the route followed by pilgrims, from the Pyrenees to Santiago de Compostela, described in 13 stages: the stages of the route, centres of population, pilgrim accommodation, peoples, rivers, customs, landscapes, relics, and the city and basilica dedicated to the Apostle St James.

Many people today are searching for these experiences of wholeness in walking, in tours and trips, on bicycles and buses. And not a few, in fact, who are exploring the local pilgrimage paths of their own countries and the broader network of ancient pilgrimage routes, find a certain meaning and way of understanding the paths their own lives have taken.

On our way through life we encounter people who point us in the right direction and people who walk alongside us; we experience what unites us and what divides us, loss and gain; we take detours and negotiate unmarked ground, as well as paths that are waymarked, well trodden or overgrown. Just as we have to scale a mountain in order to enjoy the view, we have to cross valleys and bear up in the depths of them, whether the way lies through the desert or along an asphalt motorway, through the gloom of the forest or skirting its edge, along a pilgrimage route or through life itself: each person has to find and follow his or her own way, and has to be aware of it in body, mind and spirit. The way forward makes and is made. It is the pilgrim who treads it out. Without the pilgrim, there is no path. As we are told by the Spanish poet Antonio Machado, 'You who walk, look not for the path, the path is made by your footsteps.'

Once on the way, we find new things that challenge us to risk changes. Movement and risk have something in common. The person who takes to the road weighs up and risks something. In our ways forward, characterized by our pilgrimage through daily life, risk remains mainly in the background. Once we see it in terms of 'life as a pathway', it acquires more significance. We are always having to risk leaving behind old habits in order to enter into the unknown. Being 'on the way' we risk both change and being changed ourselves.

Once on the way, there are intermediate stages. For pilgrims on the Way of St James these are like holy places, in which they experience having reached a certain spot, being welcomed and having their momentary needs and wishes satisfied. None the less this partial sense of arrival points the way towards Santiago de Compostela, where the hope of arrival is fulfilled and where medieval pilgrims held the meaning of their journeys to lie – for example, the remission of penance or the fulfilment of a vow.

Places and localities along the Way of St James are rather like the places, incidents and situations of daily life. That is, they are stages that make us more sensitive, that make us aware and make us grow towards an objective – the place of transformation.

For believers here on the pilgrimage route, Santiago de Compostela is the place in which the action of God is perceptible and the celestial Jerusalem prefigured, given that at the end of a Christian pilgrim's life, his or her culminating experience is to be united with God. That is why – as the Archbishop of Santiago, D. Julián Barrio Barrio, wrote in his Pastoral Letter for the Compostellan Holy Year 2004, *Pilgrims Through Grace* (I, 2; p. 7): 'In the night of faith and hope through which we are passing, the pilgrim to Santiago must be the watchman that announces the dawn of life after death, proclaiming faith in the resurrection and in eternal life, and makes the way of pilgrimage easy, practising the most humble virtues.'

The word 'way' seems to have a certain affinity with the word 'meaning'. To set out along the way to something suggests thinking about something, wanting to enact and experience what it means. Life is a pathway: the metaphor invites us, as seekers, to take the risk of casting off rigid modes of thought and behaviour, to move ahead, on the basis of longing, towards the meaning of our existence, and experience with all our faculties what our lives are all about.

Meanwhile, many long sections of the Way of St James are asphalt motorways, well supplied with signs and traffic signals showing what is allowed or forbidden, with indications of the speed limit and the arrangement of lanes. When we travel, whether moving along or stuck in a jam, we can experience a bit of everything: danger and stress, selfishness and deference, rudeness and courtesy. Motorways channel life, or bypass it. They impose limits, and epitomize the modern urgency to arrive and the fleetingness of human relationships. Isn't the asphalt motorway a fitting image of our lives? Realizing this is a wake-up call for us to reconsider the character and manner of human communality – on the Way of St James and in everyday life – so that we don't live only partially or on the margins.

Life as a pathway or road is an image that describes the reality of life, gives a name to its experiences and meaning to its situations. This metaphor says to us: be alert, so that life doesn't pass you by, doesn't crush you; that way, you are centred on your path, even while you move along the highways and byways of life. Be an attentive seeker on the way of life, since life is itself a pilgrims' way, and a pilgrimage along the Way of St James is a new opportunity to acknowledge it, experience it and live it. But what does it mean to go on pilgrimage?

To be a Pilgrim: Pilgrimage – What it is and What it Means

In his *Vita Nuova* (New Life), Dante distinguishes three kinds of travellers to the major holy places: the *palmieri* (palmers) who went to the Holy Land and brought back palm branches; *romei* (romeros; pilgrims to Rome) and *pellegrini* (pilgrims) who went to Galicia to pay their respects to the Apostle St James. The ancient orders of monks were also regarded as pilgrims – in other words, as strangers. Some saw themselves as pilgrims for Christ, without a fixed abode in their earthly lives. Others felt a relationship with a place (*stabilitas loci*) and placed more emphasis on their spiritual pilgrimage. What does *peregrinatio* mean in the context of the Way of St James, and what does the phrase 'life is a way' signify?

Peregrinatio is derived from the Latin word *ager*, 'field' or 'countryside' (the same term from which our word 'agriculture' is derived), and means, primarily, to go to the other side of the land (whether personal or national), to become a wanderer, to live far from home and from one's country. *Peregrinatio* is a state of being far away, of absence and, at the same time, of the process of walking, of travelling, of being 'on the road' in a foreign country. In the ancient pre-Christian era, the concept of 'being a pilgrim' had no religious overtones but, rather, legal ones. It was used to designate the stranger who did not belong to any allied state. A stranger was always the enemy, free and without legal protection. He was possibly poor and sometimes indigent, and only later on did the ancient religions develop the rule of offering hospitality to penniless strangers lacking legal protection, since they were under the special protection of the gods. In Christian terms the attribute of poverty was transferred to Jesus, who was described as a stranger who 'hath not where to lay his head' (Luke 9.58). If one gave shelter to a pilgrim, a 'wandering stranger', one gave shelter to Christ in him (see Part 6). Later, for St Francis of Assisi the figure of the 'poor pilgrim' became the ideal of Christian life in its radical adherence to the teaching of Jesus.

The Bible is full of stories about roads in which aspects of *peregrinatio* and pilgrimage are made apparent. The public life of Jesus was a strange one, lived on the move from place to place: 'I must walk today, and tomorrow, and the day following' (Luke 13.33). None the less it was the primitive monks who developed these aspects of pilgrimage clearly, and we can apply them to the Way of St James and to being on our own road through human existence. Pilgrimage should be understood in the sense of emerging, taking to the road, living in foreign parts, advancing towards and arriving at a destination.

- *Emerging*: the point at which the pilgrimage begins. Leaving one's own country was for the primitive monks the condition for being fully able to follow Jesus Christ. To leave also meant saying farewell, cutting ties and attachments, renouncing hearth and home, abandoning habits that hold one back, letting go of the past, freeing oneself of outside influences, beginning again, outwardly and inwardly. Outwardly, becoming a wandering and unknown stranger, and inwardly, on the unknown road towards one's true self, towards God.
- *Being on the road*: the primitive monks wandered from one place to another. In their external state of being on the road they wanted to remain without a country, rootless, to follow Jesus in their wandering life, and to live in the world as pilgrims going towards, as St Augustine called it, 'the

country to come'. As has already been said, to walk implies change. The person who walks moves the whole body. This frees up the spirit and the soul so that rigidity and defensiveness fall away. Being on the road externally is thus a way of advancing on the internal way. Advancing externally can further internal advance. The pilgrim does not just stay put, externally and inwardly, on the road; he experiences St Augustine's claim that 'all his life is a road, a pilgrim road to God'.

- *Living in foreign parts*: externally, but above all inwardly, this is the monastic ideal. This need not mean an actual physical state, but an interior disposition with external consequences. While today we make a pilgrimage journey to see and experience something new, the primitive monks desired above all to renew themselves inwardly in a foreign environment. On the road in a foreign country we experience new things – to which it must be added that we renew ourselves as well.

- *Going on to the very end*: the verse of Psalm 122 that cries 'Let us go unto the house of the Lord' helps us to understand the early monks' concept of being a pilgrim. Medieval pilgrims on the Way of St James also had a goal: the tomb of the Apostle in Santiago de Compostela. On the way they lived through many hardships and joys, highs and lows. Advancing towards a destination made it possible to keep their longing alight within them and at the same time to reflect upon their own lives. Originally the word 'meaning' also implied to go away, to move away, to go on a journey, to make one's way, to follow a trace, to set off in a direction. To go implies having an intention, asking the way, seeking an end. Whoever takes to the road goes on pilgrimage to find out what her or his life is based on. He or she is questioning the meaning of life.

- *Arrival*: in the house of Yahweh, or The Lord. For the early monks, earthly pilgrimage ended here; the goal of the way to God was accomplished. On the Way of St James many pilgrims reached the destination – Santiago de Compostela – but many fell by the wayside. For pilgrims, arrival could mean that their longing was fulfilled, that they experienced themselves as members of the community of pilgrims that had reached their goal, that they were in a holy place and especially close to God and his Apostle. They may even have held the event to be the most important of their lives.

Many who had already arrived perhaps could have related experiences similar to those of the two monks at the beginning of this chapter. They discovered on their outward and inward journey as pilgrims, or perhaps in their encounters with people along the way or on arrival, that they could and had to seek and find the Apostle and his Master back at home, in their daily lives. They came to understand that 'the place where the sky and the earth meet is to be found in this world, in the place that God has assigned to us.'

The experience of arriving and reaching the goal of the pilgrimage invites us to keep awake the longing for the 'heavenly Jerusalem' and to spread to others the idea of the earthly pilgrimage that leads to it.

Being a Pilgrim Changes You

In the writings of the Old and New Testaments we very often find the symbol of the road or way, above all in its ethical sense. Precepts, visions and directions demand that people walk with God according to his commandments. None the less, for the people of Israel the experience that Yahweh was a God who led them was more important. He always manifested himself anew in their wanderings. Abraham, for example, left his country, and in a long period of wandering in the company of Yahweh experienced many events that changed him and also his relationship with the deity.

What is said here of an individual was lived by Israel as a people on leaving Egypt and in the 40 years spent crossing the desert; Yahweh set them free from slavery and was their aid and comfort on the journey. The experience of the road and the experience of God were inseparably united in faith. God was only ever experienced on the march. Any experience of God brought with it movement and the loosening of ties, and led to freedom and change.

In these and other biblical narratives that focus on journeys, we can discern stages and situations from our own lives, above all their interior meaning and the question of how each person experiences and gives form to his or her state of journeying, in the religious-spiritual and the psychological senses. The biblical symbolism of the road or way aids reflection on one's own journey through life.

In the New Testament we find, in numerous narratives, Jesus Christ as a pilgrim. He took to the road to proclaim the Good News and to make people understand that God was with them. The historical accounts in the Bible are not just superficial narratives. They tell of mankind's exterior and interior journey, of the meaning and centre of human existence. They speak in images about the ways of change. Change means that in the first place everything that exists is good, but that many things alter our being and our true selves. To change would consist, then, in reshaping the original image and extracting it from the jumble of images we carry within us. In change there is the aspect of grace. God changes a person while he or she is on their life's journey. A well-known biblical example in which we can see in action the external and internal state of being 'on the way' is the encounter with the risen Christ (as yet unrecognized) and the change brought about in the two disciples in the story of the road to Emmaus (Luke 24.13–25). (See also Part 7.)

To be on the way on the route taken by pilgrims to Santiago de Compostela can bring about change. This is made clear in two poems drawn from very different sources but attesting to the same reality:

To the Pilgrim

Go
    from the day of your birth
    you have been on the journey.

Go

    an encounter awaits you
    with whom?
    perhaps with your own self.

Go

    your steps will be your words
    the journey your song
    your fatigue your prayer
    and your silence will at last speak.

Go

    with the others
    but out of yourself
    you that think yourself surrounded by unfriendliness
    will find joy.

Go

    although your spirit may not know where
    your feet will carry your heart.

Go

    another is coming to meet you,
    and is searching for you
    so that you can find Him in the sanctuary
    at the end of the pilgrimage,
    in the sanctuary deep inside your heart.

'He Is Your Peace, He Is Your Peace', carried by a South African pilgrim and presented at Refugio Gaucelmo.

A Message to Pilgrims

Brother pilgrim,
Come to the sanctuary,
'March towards the splendour.
Your God goes with you.'

Prepare your heart
To travel
With joy and confidence,
Alone or with your brothers,
But come.

Follow the way
Marked out long ago
Whoever you are;
There is a corner for you in
The Father's house . . .

If you are thirsty for love,
For peace, for happiness,
For forgiveness and for justice,
Come to draw the water
From the springs of salvation.

Young and full of passion
Or old and wracked
With suffering,
You who feel
Excluded,
Or who enjoy the sweetness
Of family life.

Let the light
Of the Gospels shine on you.

Look,
And come back reconciled,
Comforted, renewed.

Announce the Good News, then,
To your brothers.
God loves us
And is waiting for us.

March towards the splendour.
Your God goes with you.

From a wall in the monastery of Lluc, Majorca,
translated by Janet Richardson

On the way, on the road to Santiago – whether as a pilgrim on foot or on a bicycle or by some other means, alone or in a group, perhaps in a bus – you are invited to explore the route, to experience its meaning, to change and be changed. This is the aim of the pilgrim's journey along the Way of St James and along the road of his or her life. It is hoped that the thoughts, extracts and encouragement offered here will motivate and accompany you on that journey.

> We are pilgrims, and we are all heading for the same place by different roads.
>
> *Antoine de Saint-Exupéry*

The Structure of this Book – the Pilgrim's *Vademecum*

The material is organized thematically in 15 parts, each of which begins with a brief description of the places that are interesting to visit and to get to know along the Spanish part of the Way of St James, which extends from the Pyrenees to Santiago de Compostela, with an extension to Cape Finisterre. Then, in consecutive sub-sections, the chosen theme is developed, providing food for thought and the historical, anthropological and religious background appropriate to each part. To these are added brief texts that may serve to awaken a more profound personal response.

The distribution of themes, as one would expect, follows the journey along the *Camino*, and progression in the pilgrimage has been anticipated in the 15 parts that trace the physical Way of St James.

If you want to undertake part or all of the route on the basis of one part per day, you will obviously have to do the part in question or the whole journey by mechanized means. Even so, it may not be possible to complete a single stretch in one day. It's up to each person to decide how much time to allow. Of course, without being critical of other ways of doing the *Camino*, we suggest that the best way of doing it is on foot.

We realize, however, that not everyone is in a position to do this, and the *Camino* has much to teach us all. The text of this book, in its simplicity, seeks to point the way for any reader and to be an aid to knowing, understanding and internalizing the Way of St James.

Each part is organized within the following sections:

- **Theme** – indicated by the title of the part.
- **The Route** – the places along the route and their context are presented, with an outline of the surviving monuments and their history. This is important for awakening interest in the theme in all its aspects.
- **Stop and Think About It** – these sections offer concepts, ideas, reflections and quoted material to support the theme.
- **Between Past and Present** – information and explanations are given as aids to seeing and understanding the places discussed, as well as the themes and questions, from a religious, artistic, historical and cultural point of view.

Part 1
Setting Out for Santiago

THE ROUTE

From Your Own Front Door to the Camino

At your own front door. This is your departure point: the decision to travel the Way of St James is in a sense the point at which the journey begins. You begin to prepare yourself, through reading, looking at photographs, any other means – and by talking to people and/or pilgrims who know the route in one way or another. You start learning about history, culture, art, religion, customs. However you cover the distance between home and the *Camino*, the starting point on any pilgrimage to Santiago is your own front door. The Way always begins at your own front door.

➡ The traditional *Camino de Santiago* is the main branch, and is also often called the *Camino Francés* since it was the route taken and populated by the French, and became known as such all over Europe. We will begin at the pass of Ibañeta, a little before Roncesvalles, and at the pass of the Somport, before Jaca.

➡ There were and are other routes, some with variants, to Santiago de Compostela in the Iberian peninsula: the *Camino del Norte* – considered the earliest – which runs along the Cantabrian coast and through Oviedo, or which, from Pamplona and Victoria-Gasteiz to Santillana del Mar, then proceeds to Oviedo. From Victoria-Gasteiz one can go directly to Burgos (this is the old Roman road from Bordeaux to Astorga) or to Santo Domingo de la Calzada, to join the *Camino Francés*. The *Via de la Plata*, also known as the *Camino Mozarabe*, reaches Santiago from Seville by way of Mérida, Cáceres, Salamanca and Astorga, uniting there with the *Camino Francés*, or veering left at Zamora to take the route through the north of Portugal or through Benavente, Sanabria and Orense. There are others from the Levant and Catalunya that are also becoming more frequently travelled, and there is the sea route from the British Isles to La Coruña, from which pilgrims then walked to Santiago along the short but historic *Camino Inglés*.

The Pilgrim Blessing

Before the medieval pilgrims coming from their respective countries – or together, from one of the cities that were gathering points – set off on their pilgrimages, they had to have paid their debts, made their wills, been to confession and attended Mass. Only then could they be sent off on pilgrimage. In 1078 there already existed the pilgrim blessing that is still imparted today at Roncesvalles:

The Pilgrim Blessing

May the Lord direct your steps with His blessing and be your inseparable companion along the Way.

May the Holy Virgin Mary grant you her maternal protection, defend you from bodily and spiritual danger, and may you be gathered safely under her mantle at the end of your pilgrimage.

May the Archangel St Raphael accompany you every step of the way, as he accompanied Tobias, and keep you safe from all harm and ill-fortune.

Oh God, who brought Abraham out of the city of Ur of the Chaldees, protecting him in all his pilgrim wanderings, and who guided the Hebrews in their journey across the desert, we beg you to bless these your servants who, for love of your name now go as pilgrims to Santiago de Compostela.

Be for them companion on the journey, signpost at the crossroads, encouragement in weariness, defence when dangers threaten, refuge on the way, shade in the heat, light in the darkness, comfort in discouragement and firmness in their resolve, that with your aid, Lord, they may arrive without harm at their journey's end and, enriched in graces and virtues, return safely to their homes that ache for their return, filled with healing and perpetual joy. For the sake of Jesus Christ, Our Lord. Amen.

STOP AND THINK ABOUT IT

'The longest journey in the world begins with a single step.' This Chinese proverb reminds us of something that is often forgotten: every journey, exterior or interior, begins from the beginning, and in order for us to feel comfortable these two important aspects must be in harmony. Remember the anecdote about the globetrotter (see pp. xiii–xiv). Modern means of transport can cover great distances rapidly. We too are therefore in danger of arriving at our destination more rapidly in body than in spirit. It's worth pausing a moment now, at the beginning, to reflect on how we set out on our journey.

Leaving to go on a Journey – Setting off

To set off means:

- In the first instance, we begin to make a thought, an idea or a wish into a reality. At the beginning, perhaps, we are alone; later we become aware that others have entertained similar thoughts and longings. We set off together, taking the first step, just as we do on the Way itself, towards Santiago de Compostela.

- Some decisions are taken spontaneously, others are weighed up more carefully. To do the *Camino* it's better to think about it and plan the route and the journey. Little by little one begins assimilating the idea, inwardly and outwardly. It's best to decide what you will need and to try out your equipment and rucksack, to gauge your physical condition, though without undue worry about this.

- We are leaving family and professional obligations behind, at least for a certain time, as well as doing without the usual routine, relationships, surroundings and so on. At the same time we open ourselves to the new things and people that we may meet on the Way of St James. Departure, setting off, makes me see that the inward state of being on the way is possibly cramped in the daily life I lead. Perhaps it may be possible to live it differently, or more vividly, on the *Camino*.

- We are on the way in the company of others, together. There is always something still to be settled. We know the travel schedule and the route plan; we have taught ourselves about the art, the history and the culture of the *Camino*. But a degree of uncertainty lingers. It's understood that those participating will introduce themselves, each when the moment seems right. Setting off for Santiago de Compostela offers the chance to pool information, uniting it to personal experience; to get to know something about the medieval and religious context of the pilgrimage – for example, the reasons that motivated pilgrims, the figure of St James, the religious importance of the Way, the influence of the Moorish period in Spain – and therefore to begin to assimilate it. Along with all of this comes the invitation to see things with a fresh eye, to reflect on what is seen, and at the same time to discern the hints from the past that will help us to see clearly our own situation of being 'on the way' in our daily life, to understand it and, if necessary, to change it.

- In the Bible there are many stories involving setting off or departures – for example, that of Abraham, who at God's command struck and moved his tents on the sole basis of a promise. This and other scriptural narratives involving journeys invite us to experience what it means to demand something of oneself, to risk something and commit oneself to something. Trusting in God, Abraham risks embarking on the journey and sets off; he does not seek assurance, he just goes.

- The first step has been taken. This book invites you to live and enjoy the whole length of the Way of St James in all its rich and varied culture, history, art, landscape and religious sense. To do this involves reflection on the inner state of being 'on the way', and engagement on a personal level and a communal one in the experience of being on the road, extending yourself to others and seeking with them this kind of communal experience – the kind that was also important to the pilgrims of past centuries.

- We are not 'on the way' only on this journey. Life in its entirety will have many stages, each with its own starting point. We are always trying to set off again, externally and internally. A journey along the *Camino* is one such stage, but a particularly significant one that can provide us with insight and strength for the rest of our lives.

Leaving

Departures without arrival,
Journeys without a goal:
We walking wounded
Celebrate: find
Wholeness in the incomplete.

For parting holds a promise,
And movement, a quenching of the raging
Thirst for otherness –
This is the choice of change.

In winter though, when ice
Outlines the landscape's ribs,
And even skeletons are cold . . .
The spirit too is held by frost
And waymarks beckon, but in vain.

Be still, and see:
The clods already harrowed.
The young lamb staggers
On the withered grass.

Close the door, hide the key.
A last look over the garden wall –
Already on the road, a stranger,
With compass and with cockleshell,
And the wind's caress.

> *

For the pilgrim
Home lies between
The familiar places;
Friends are people
You leave behind;
Conversation the silent voice
Of a long-buried cockleshell;
Love is the wind's
Cold caress,
And fame is to pass by,
Unnoticed.

On the journey into exile,
The moon's above Orion, bright,
And cathedral spires glow still
In Sirius' blue light.

Midnight, and in the space between the chimes,
I sense the space between the stars.
Brief moments, vanishing –
In letting go, we find what's ours.

> *

Go lightly, pilgrim, on this ancient earth
And when you can, alone.
In wind and rain find all your mirth,
And in the silence make your home.

Howard Nelson

BETWEEN PAST AND PRESENT

Many Roads and One Way

We are told in Book V (the *Pilgrim's Guide*) of the *Codex Calixtinus*: 'There are four roads to Santiago that in Puente la Reina in Spain join to become one.' The *Via Turonensis* from Paris, via Orléans, Tours and Poitiers to Ostabat; the *Via Lemovicensis* from Vézelay, through Limoges and Perigueux to Ostabat; the *Via Podensis* from Le Puy, Conques and Moissac to Ostabat: these three, coming together at Ostabat, continue as one route over the pass of Ibañeta to Roncesvalles and Pamplona, and from there to Puente la Reina. The fourth road, the *Via Tolosana*, leaves from Arles and goes by way of Toulouse to the Somport Pass and Jaca. In Puente la Reina it meets the road coming from Pamplona to form the *Camino Francés*, or 'French Way', which then carries pilgrims to Santiago via Estella, Logroño, Burgos, León, Astorga and Ponferrada.

The brief description of the four pilgrim roads through France in Book V of the *Liber Sancti Jacobi* is silent on the subject of other routes or shortcuts. Leaving aside the places where German pilgrims gathered before setting off to join one of the routes through France, such as Aachen and Einsiedeln, it is known that pilgrims from England and the Baltic often went by sea to the French coast (to the city of Bordeaux, for example) or reached landfall in Spain at La Coruña, Padrón or Noya. From the south of Spain pilgrims took the *Via de la Plata*, a broad Roman road built from the sea, with slave labour, through Mérida, Salamanca and Zamora to Santiago, either directly, through Orense, or linking up with the *Camino Francés* in Astorga.

The most travelled routes were the four principal ones mentioned, but there also arose lateral routes, shortcuts and detours, with their own monasteries, churches and inns.

Before the eleventh century, the first part of the *Camino* in Spain ran further north, generally along the coast so as to protect pilgrims from Muslim attack, or by way of the ancient Roman road that went from Bordeaux via Pamplona and/or Vitoria-Gasteiz to Astorga. From Vitoria-Gasteiz a road also went by way of Santillana del Mar to Oviedo, continuing along the *Camino del Norte*. Sancho 'el Mayor' (1000–35) laid down what later became the 'classical' route to Santiago from Pamplona to Nájera, for economic, religious and tactical reasons, once the Muslim occupation of that region had ended. The goal of pilgrims was the tomb of St James, but they also visited other sacred places: for example, the monastery of Santo Domingo de Silos, which although a detour was allowed for in the plans of many pilgrims as a welcome opportunity to rest, pray and ask the favours of a local saint.

St James and St John in brotherly dispute: Sarmental doorway, Burgos Cathedral.

In Burgos Cathedral is a frieze of Apostles showing St James and St John in brotherly dispute. Each of them is shown with a book of sacred Scripture. Two of them, the young one in the middle and his neighbour on the right, seem to be arguing. John, with the open book, is indicating a text to his brother James, as though trying to convince him of its meaning. But James, completely calm and certain, shows him the cover of his book, which is covered with scallop-shells, the emblem of the pilgrimage to his shrine.

What is he trying to say? Without doubt, that the Word is valid, but in addition, here, 'We are on the way! The way of seeking leads to Christ and the Word is part of this.' In being on the way one becomes a seeker. The shell is the symbol of being open to the Way.

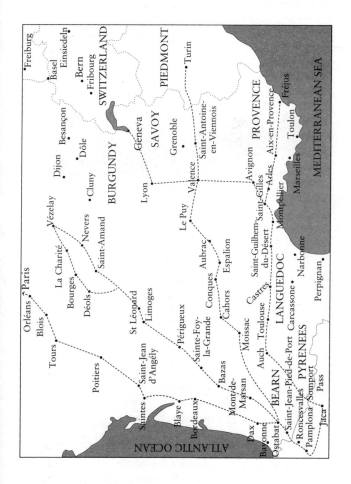

*The four major routes through France, leading to the Way of
St James in Spain*

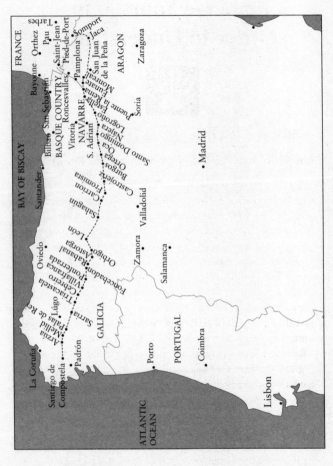

The most popular Way of St James, or Camino de Santiago, in Spain.
This route is also known as the Camino Francés.

Part 2
Immerse Yourself in
Order to Understand

THE ROUTE

From Saint-Jean-Pied-de-Port to Puente la Reina

➡ Leaving Saint-Jean-Pied-de-Port, the route enters the Pyrenees by way of Arnegui/Arnegi and ascends through Valcarlos (the Valley of Charlemagne)/Luzaide, to reach the highest point (1,057 metres) at the pass of Ibañeta, where the monastery of San Salvador once stood, and where today there is a modern chapel with a bell to orient pilgrims. A monumental stone recalls the historic and emblematic poem, the *Song of Roland*, although the geographical context places the action in the narrow gorge of the Urrobi river. The Provençal troubadour called the enemy 'Saracens', when in fact the attack was mounted by the Navarrese Basques of the region.

➡ Roncesvalles/Orreaga: in the valley stands the Real Colegiata de Santa María, still held by the Augustinians: thirteenth-century church, with statue known as the Virgen de Roncesvalles (thirteenth to fourteenth centuries), chapter room (fourteenth century), tomb of Sancho 'el Fuerte' of Navarre (fourteenth century), chapels of Santiago (thirteenth century) and Sancti Spiritus (also known as the 'Silo de Carlomagno'); there is a museum in the lower part, where Roland was buried and, later, pilgrims. Documents of 1127 mention the founding of a pilgrim hospital that is still operating today. Pilgrims can stay there for up to three days. Leaving for Santiago, you pass a fourteenth-century pilgrims' cross.

➡ The Way leads to Burguete/Auritz and leaves the Urrobi river to the left, crossing a small Romanesque bridge and continuing to Espinal/Auritzburri, founded in 1269 by Teobaldo II of Navarre. It runs on through Viscarret/Biscarret and Linzoain on the Alto de Erro. In Zubiri (the 'place of the bridge') it crosses a Gothic bridge over the river Arga.

➡ Larrasoaña, with its fourteenth-century bridge, already had an Augustinian monastery in the eleventh century that became a dependency of Leyre in 1087. A place of great jacobean tradition, it was legally designated a French settlement in 1174.

➡ The route continues through Zuriain, Iroz and Arleta to the valley of Azcabarte, where the basilica of Trinidad de Arre – with a long tradition of hospitality to pilgrims – stands by the river. It then carries on through Vilava and Burlada and so reaches Pamplona.

➡ Pamplona/Iruña: named for the Roman politician and general Pompey, AD 106–46, who founded it in AD 70. It has been an episcopal see since the sixth century. Occupied during the Muslim invasions, it was liberated by Charlemagne in 778. Capital of the ancient kingdom of Navarre until it became part of Castile in 1512, it granted special protection and privileges to pilgrims. Notable monuments: Romanesque church of San Sernín or Saturnino (rebuilt thirteenth century) with a statue of Santiago and a pilgrim in the entrance and an eighteenth-century chapel of the Virgen del Camino, patroness of the city. Metropolitan cathedral of Santa María la Real (fourteenth–sixteenth centuries; the Romanesque one was destroyed by fire in 1390), with eighteenth-century main door by Ventura Rodríguez; lady chapel with seated twelfth-century image of the Virgin; fifteenth-century alabaster mausoleum of Carlos II 'el Noble' of Navarre; fourteenth-century doorway to the cloister known as 'La Puerta Preciosa' (the beautiful doorway); beyond it lie the Barbazana chapel, the diocesan museum, the cellars, kitchens and pilgrims' dining-room. Other city monuments include the Magdalena bridge, city walls, gate known as the Puerta de Francia, streets (such as the ancient Rúa de los Peregrinos and Dormitalería) by which the Way of St

James passes through the city, the citadel, Plaza del Castillo, town hall and other municipal buildings, including the town museum. Ignatius of Loyola (1494–1556), the founder of the Jesuits, was wounded here in 1521 fighting against the French. In a chapel of the church of San Lorenzo there is a much-loved statue of San Fermín, patron of the city, whose festival (7 July) is characterized by the famous running of the bulls, immortalized by Ernest Hemingway in his novel *Fiesta*.

→ The route carries on through Cizur, Guendulain and Zariquiegui, passing close to the fountain of 'la Reniega' (Renunciation) in the ascent to the Alto del Perdon (780 metres). It then descends to Uterga, Muruzábal and Obanos, where the 'Mystery of Obanos', a play enacted annually by local people, recalls the story of St Felicia and her brother St William. It continues to the point where the monument of a pilgrim indicates the union of the roads from Somport and Roncesvalles, a little before Puente la Reina.

Stop and Think About It

The medieval pilgrim had to direct himself to one of the recognized gathering places and from there reach the route and what it offered. Today's possibilities for travel mean that distance is no longer a barrier, and we can reach the route with relative ease. Undoubtedly, many of the experiences acquired by pilgrims setting off on foot are being lost, although today's modes of transport are allowing many others to discover the history, ambience and spirituality of the Way of St James in their own manner. We must accept that not everyone enjoys the physical and psychological ability to take to the road just like that. On the other hand, a route or trip that is well thought out and prepared can impart a great deal of understanding to both individuals and groups. However it is managed, for this to happen there should be sufficient time for impressions to sink in and for reflection.

Immerse Yourself in Being on the *Camino*

A tap in the medieval village of Borce in the Aspe valley: a welcome sight for the pilgrim.

It may be that you are already on the *Camino* – you have set out, you may be about to do so or maybe you just want to think about it, partly by reading this section. You are on it in some way or other, and even if only mentally it's a good idea to embrace the fact, sinking yourself in the reality of it as fully as you can. If you don't you'll find yourself literally out of step. Don't be afraid or suspicious: there's nothing sectarian or one-sided about it. The aim is that you should see more, and better. On this Way we have a companion: Santiago the son of Zebedee, also called the Son of Thunder. This is the Apostle St James, and through him will come Jesus – or possibly the other way round. For the moment, here and now, we have a biblical text concerning the way St James came to take to the road with Jesus of Nazareth: 'And when he had gone a little farther thence, he saw James the son of Zebedee, and John his brother, who also were in the ship mending their nets. And straightway he called them: and they left their father Zebedee in the ship with the hired servants, and went after him' (Mark 1.19–20). This text about calling or vocation may awaken in us a certain resistance. From our point of view it is earth-shaking – to leave work and family and follow the summons of a rabbi. What fascination this man must have exercised, so to affect the wishes and longings of other human beings as to uproot them from their everyday existence and show them the perspectives of another way of life!

In the meeting with him they must have felt the urge to make a decision, for 'the time is fulfilled' (Mark 1.15) in which there may be more humanity and justice, freedom and a new beginning. That is why it is worth leaving everything. There is another calling and vocation more essential than that of a fisherman. None the less, we know they continued to be fishermen but that their work acquired a new quality. Jesus later called them 'fishers of men'. They were to live his message in their dealings with others and invite them to do the same.

St James the Great belonged from the very beginning to the inner circle of Jesus' disciples. In his first meeting with Jesus he found his vocation. Perhaps somewhat prepared for it by the preaching of repentance on the part of John the Baptist, he became a seeker and a follower of Jesus.

We too are on the way, we are seekers on the way that bears the name of the Apostle. A Chinese folktale illustrates the manner in which we can allow ourselves to enter and become submerged in the Way of St James.

A little figurine made of salt, after a long trek through dry regions, came to the sea, which it had never seen before. It stood on the bank and scanned the strangely agitated surface. To its question as to what this was, there came back the answer, 'I am the sea.' The salt figurine replied, 'What is that – the sea?' The sea answered, 'That is what I am.' Then the figurine said, 'I can't understand it, however much I would like to. I simply don't know how.' The sea said, 'Touch me, and then you will understand me.' The salt figurine extended its foot and touched the sea. It felt a strange sensation: this strange being began to be recognizable. The figurine withdrew its foot and saw that its toes had disappeared. 'What have you done?' it cried, horrified. The sea replied, 'You've had to let go of something in order to understand me.' Little by little the salt figurine was dissolving into the sea. At the same time it had the feeling that it understood the sea more and more.

Touch and permit yourself to be touched in order to give something, let yourself enter and be submerged in order to understand and comprehend. This is the invitation made by this story to your state of being on the way on the road to Santiago de Compostela. You can study it and explore it using some form of vehicle or on foot, and live it through its multiple expressions, in history, art and culture. The tourist's lively eyes and awakened curiosity are important and useful. None the less, the decisive thing is whether you, on immersing yourself in the *Camino de Santiago*, understand its meaning, whether it revives the interior *Camino* of your life and whether your search takes on a new orientation.

Thou art the Journey and the Journey's End

O Father, give the spirit power to climb
To the fountain of all light, and be purified.
Break through the mists of earth, the weight of the clod,
Shine forth in splendour, thou that art calm weather,
And quiet resting place for faithful souls.
To see thee is the end and the beginning,
Thou carriest us, and thou dost go before,
Thou art the journey, and the journey's end.

Boethius (480–524)

BETWEEN PAST AND PRESENT

Calle de la Dormitalería – *Pilgrim, be on Your Guard*

Along the Way of St James the pilgrim inns and hospitals were looked after by the confraternities and the religious communities. However, in Pamplona the responsible authority was the Cathedral. The chapter, together with the bishop, charged one of the canons with this task. Here pilgrims encountered special protection and dedication, and Pamplona was known for its generous portions of bread and wine and its good cuisine. The lands next to the Cathedral were given over to the support of pilgrims as well as to the relief of the poor and socially marginalized. In 1835 the State confiscated the possessions of the charitable foundations, but their ancient dedication and purpose is commemorated in the old street name: *Calle de la Dormitalería*; that is, the street where pilgrims could find rest. But there was an important distinction: they were not to sleep, but to remain alert.

What is known today about relaxation exercises indicates that this kind of half-sleep produces, on the one hand, a deep easing of physical tension and, on the other, a heightened spiritual alertness. Pilgrims were invited to adopt this state in the *Dormitalería*. As pilgrims to Santiago, on the road, they had to rest so as to replenish their physical and spiritual strength. Nevertheless they were not supposed to fall into deep slumber. They were supposed to rest by dozing, half asleep and half awake so that they didn't miss the moment of departure and were always ready to resume the journey. Their existence as pilgrims and their attitude while on the *Camino de Santiago* is therefore an image of the road of life as it really is. On earth you are on the road; here you can only sleep lightly or doze. We have to be alert, 'for ye know neither the day nor the hour' (Matt. 25.13) when Christ opens the gate to final rest in the Kingdom of God.

A street sign in Pamplona recalls the pilgrimage.

Dormitalería also means to be awake to the realities and the signs of God in the world so that they do not go unnoticed. As is indicated by the name of the street, given in Castilian Spanish and in Basque, assistance to pilgrims was the responsibility of the 'canon of the dormitory'. He looked after pilgrims and the place prepared for their rest. Together with concern for the pilgrims' bodily well-being (such as the food they were given), care was also expended on their spiritual welfare so that watchful and strengthened in body and spirit they could carry on towards the city of the Apostle.

Part 3
About the *Camino* from *Alpha* to *Omega*

THE ROUTE

From the Somport Pass to Puente la Reina

➜ The Somport Pass (*Summus Portus*): the pass (1,631 metres) of the *Via Tolosana* that runs from Arles via Toulouse, Oloron Sainte-Marie and Jaca to Puente la Reina, where all roads meet to become one, according to the *Codex Calixtinus*.

➜ Santa Cristina: the *Codex Calixtinus* named it as one of the three most important hospitals in the world, serving pilgrims, the poor and the sick.

Waymarking along the Camino *ranges from the simple yellow arrows painted by volunteers to the stone markers set up by local authorities.*

➡ The way continues through Canfranc (*Campus Francus*) with its pre-twelfth-century hospital, Vilanúa, which is cited in documents before the tenth century, and Aruej, with its eleventh-century church, reaching Castiello de Jaca and, finally, Jaca.

➡ Jaca: one of the most historic cities in Spain. Following the Iberians' struggle against the Romans, the domination of the latter continued, ceding to that of the Visigoths and, later, the Moors. The new era was marked by the rule of Ramíro, Count of Aragón and son of Sancho III 'el Mayor' of Navarre, and the code of law granted in 1063. In this period the cathedral dedicated to San Pedro was built (1060); it houses the relics of San Indalecio (Bishop of Urci, Almeria, Auca, Villafranca Montes de Oca and Burgos), of one of the seven *varones Apostólicos* (apostolic young men) who are supposed to have accompanied St James to Spain, and those of St Felix and St Voto (Odón), the founders of the monastery of San Juan de la Peña. The cathedral has a west door bearing the *chi-rho*; in the cloister is the diocesan museum, with an excellent collection of Romanesque frescos. The cathedral of Jaca was the first church in Spain built in the Burgundian Romanesque style, and the notable brickwork set the style for almost all the other Romanesque churches in the country. Other important monuments in Jaca are the citadel (sixteenth century), the bridge of San Miguel and the church of Santiago, with its tomb of Doña Sancha, daughter of Ramíro I.

➡ It's a good idea to acquaint yourself, even if only by reading, with two important places nearby. First, Santa Cruz de la Serós, a town with a pre-Romanesque church (San Caprasio, ninth to eleventh centuries) and the convent church of Santa María (Serós derives from the Latin *sorores*, or sisters) dating from the twelfth century and founded by Doña Sancha, with a four-storied tower and a crismon on the west door. Second, San Juan de la Peña, a monastery dating from the eighth century. The brothers Voto and Felix, fleeing from the Muslims, reached this spot where there lived a hermit called Juan, and established an eremitical community. It was given its present name by Sancho 'el Mayor' in 1025; the rest of the holy brotherhood is venerated in the cathedral in Jaca. The monastery enjoyed its greatest splendour in the period from 1071, when the Cluniac reform was introduced into Spain. From 2 March – Ash Wednesday – of that year, the new Liturgy of the Hours approved by Rome began to be used and the old style hitherto favoured by Toledo was phased out. King Sancho Ramírez and the papal legate were present to witness this solemn break with tradition. Other monuments include: remains of the tenth-century Mozarabic and pre-Romanesque church, eleventh-century council chamber, twelfth-century cloister, and royal pantheon with the cross belonging to the first king of Navarre, Iñigo Arista. For a time the vessel believed to be the Holy Grail was kept here. Pope Sixtus II, in the reign of the Emperor Valeriano (253–8), allowed it to be taken during an outbreak of persecution to the church of San Lorenzo in his own city of Huesca, and it was brought here during the Moorish occupation; later, thanks to Pope Clement VII (1378–94) and St Vincent Ferrer, in 1416 it was transferred to Valencia. In the eighteenth century another monastery was built on the mountain above, but is of lesser artistic value.

➡ The Way continues through Santa Cilia de Jaca to Puente de la Reina de Jaca. The Yesa reservoir, which dams the river Arga, divides the route, one part running along its left side through almost or totally abandoned places like Arrés, Martes, Mianos, Artieda, Ruesta and Undués de Lerda, to Sangüesa. The way to the right is easier and safer, and goes by way of Berdún, Sigüés, Esco and Tiermas (a place of hot sulphur springs) to Yesa. From there you can visit Leyre.

➡ Monastery of San Salvador de Leyre/Leire: there has been a Benedictine community here since 1954 but the monastery dates from Visigothic times and is mentioned in 848 by San Eulogio of Cordoba, who visited it. At times it has been monastery, episcopal see, royal court and pantheon of the Navarrese kings, as well as the refuge of kings and bishops during the Moorish domination. Leyre achieved its greatest splendour in the eleventh and twelfth centuries. Sancho III 'el Mayor' (1000–35) endowed it with great privileges. The pre-Romanesque crypt (ninth to eleventh centuries) is dedicated to San Babil, who was martyred in the reign of the Emperor Decius (third century). The church was enlarged in the eleventh, twelfth and fourteenth centuries and has a beautiful doorway (the *Porta Speciosa*, eleventh and twelfth centuries), with central column, tympanum and archivolts. In the church is a reliquary containing the remains of the kings of Navarre. Confiscated by the state in 1835, the buildings were given new life with the arrival of the Benedictines in 1954. The interesting legend of San Virila is associated with Leyre: enraptured by the song of a bird, the saint wandered in the garden of the monastery for 300 years without noticing the passage of time: a reference to eternity.

➡ Javier/Xabier: St Francis Xavier, the co-founder (with St Ignatius of Loyola) of the Jesuits and missionary to the Far East, was born in the eleventh-century castle with its prominent tower.

➡ Sangüesa/Zangoza: St Francis of Assisi fell ill in Rocaforte on his way to Santiago; Alfonso I 'el Batallador' granted the pre-Romanesque town its charter in 1122. The church of San Francisco with its cloister dates from the thirteenth to the sixteenth centuries; the twelfth- and thirteenth-century church of Santiago has a sixteenth-century statue of 'Santiago peregrino' and, facing the church, the old rectory houses a cultural centre. Other buildings of note include the *ayuntamiento*, the ruins of the palace of the kings of Navarre, and the church of Santa María la Real, with an excellent twelfth- and thirteenth-century doorway and, inside, a sixteenth-century image of Our Lady of Rocamadour.

➡ The Way continues through Liédana (given by Sancho III 'el Mayor' to Leyre), passing close to the ruins of a Roman villa and the Foz de Lumbier/Iruberri, and then ascends the Alto de Loiti (728 metres). Some guides show it as going by way of the Alto de Aibar, Izco and Abinzano, then Salinas de Ibargoiti and Monreal, crossing the latter's medieval bridge over the river Elorz. Its castle, now vanished, was evidence of its importance as a town settled by the French, rather like Estella, with the support of King García Ramírez.

➡ The Way passes through Yarnoz, Tiebas, Campanas,

Enériz (or as alternatives, Muruarte de Reta and Olcoz), then Eunate, Obanos and Puente la Reina, where it meets the route from Roncesvalles. An iron statue of Santiago as a pilgrim, and an evocative plaque, mark the spot.

→ Santa María de Eunate (also known as the 'Virgin of the Hundred Doors'), the isolated church, in whose vicinity pilgrims' mortal remains have been found, is modelled on the church of the Holy Sepulchre in Jerusalem. The theological symbolism of its architecture shows it to be an 'Ascension church', similar to that of the Mount of Olives. Some authorities ascribe it to the Order of St John of Jerusalem (twelfth century), and suggest that the Templars were also active here. Eunate is a Basque name: *eun* is 'a hundred' and *atea* is 'door'; the name has also appeared as 'Onat', 'good door', or 'Unat', the door to infinity (symbolized by the building's octagonal shape) or to eternity; there is nothing more infinite than the eternal. From the standpoint of faith, the experience of death for the Christian was like a liberation from this 'vale of tears'. Thus there is a parallel between the death of the Christian and Jesus' ascension into heaven: we come from God and we return to him. Our true home is not of this world. We are here only fleetingly, as guests, and therefore pilgrims from the earthly realm on the way to the heavenly one, to the house of the Father. On the inner surface of the cupola everything is directed to a central point, symbolizing Christ. The octagonal shape of the building is rimmed by an octagonal parade of arches. The roof is topped by a small spire that earlier served as a lantern, as at Torres del Rio. Nearby stands the ancient (thirteenth-century) hospital.

STOP AND THINK ABOUT IT

Freed from the obligations of our everyday lives, being on the Way of St James opens to us the opportunity to rediscover and foster a certain ability that may be a little rusty. This ability, or rather approach to things, is admiration. We explain, we understand, we reflect, we set priorities. But if we really want to experience the richness of life, the symbols and the spirit of the Way of St James, we need to learn first of all to admire. Here is a story that offers food for thought.

On the Road Early, Full of Admiration

A learned man was travelling in the desert and took with him some Muslim guides. At sunset the Muslims spread out their mats on the ground to pray. 'What are you doing?' he asked one of them. 'Praying.' 'To whom?' 'To Allah.' 'Have you ever seen him, touched him, heard him?' 'No.' 'Well, you're daft, then!' On the following morning, when the learned man emerged from his tent, he said to one of the Muslims: 'There's been a camel here, in the night!' The Muslim's eyes sparkled: 'Did you see it, touch it, hear it?' 'No.' 'Then how do you know, wise as you are?' The learned man replied, 'You can see its tracks, all around the tent.' Meanwhile, the sun was rising in all its splendour. The Muslim pointed and said 'There you see the tracks left by Allah.'

We come across the 'tracks left by God' everywhere: in the rising sun, in the beauty of nature, in energy, in a flower growing along the roadside, in the infinity of the night sky, in the face of another person. The story reminds us that all created things are like an image of God. In creation we can recognize this and encounter it, given that, unlike the 'learned man', we can use our eyes, we can open the doors and windows of our senses and let ourselves be carried away by admiration, to an encounter with life in all its diversity. To admire is a receptive approach. In the Bible we often find men who admire the works of God – admire, because they cannot fully grasp them with their understanding. To admire means to open oneself, to be alert with all one's senses, to see what lies beyond, to see with the heart, to listen to the intuitions of the soul, to trust them and not to drown them out at once with dry logic.

The Way of St James is a gift, to help us recognize the signs of God in the world and to exercise admiration on our way through its different landscapes, in our encounters with people, in the traces left behind by pilgrims up ahead, in the religious symbolism of the *Camino*, in its history and the ways art finds expression. And in art itself! Here we shall only refer to the *chi-rho* (see the following section) as a sign to watch for on the *Camino de Santiago*. It unites an ancient symbol for the sun with the sign for Christ, and changes the usual manner of reading the letters *alpha* (A-a) and *omega* (Ω-o). Like the sun (Christ), we are on the way of pilgrimage from east (A) to west (Ω), to the tomb of the Apostle. Being on pilgrimage here is only a symbol of the pilgrimage of our lives, in which Christ accompanies us. With admiration, we discern in such artistic symbols on the Way of St James the faith and hope of mankind.

We are invited to admire. Being on the *Camino* we are offered favourable occasions in which faith can grow. Or rather, in the words of Brother Roger, the founder of Taizé, we might say: learn all over again to admire, and 'live what you have acknowledged through faith – but really live it'.

BETWEEN PAST AND PRESENT

The Chi-Rho – *the Monogram of Jesus that Accompanies You on the* Camino

Along the Way of St James we frequently find the monogram of Christ known as the *chi-rho* or *labarum*. We find it very early on, after coming down from the Somport Pass, in Jaca, on the tympanum of the oldest Romanesque cathedral on Spanish soil, and shortly thereafter in Santa Cruz de la Serós, in San Juan de la Peña in the royal pantheon, in the side chapel of the monastery church at Leyre, in the portico of the church of San Román in Cirauqui, and repeatedly all the way to the Plaza de las Platerías of the cathedral of Santiago de Compostela. Its frequent use indicates that the monogram is an important sign on the Way of St James, although it was already known very early – for example, in Rome in the third century and then in other places, with many variants – in Christian art. Its specific meaning on the Way of St James is the result of the deliberate use of signs of abbreviation. Before looking at it more closely there are a few basic things to remember about it. Monograms are abbreviations of a name that unite two or more letters to form a sign. Together with the practical reasons for this they also were important signs of reverence; for example, those signifying the name of Jesus or Christ. Certain holy names were condensed into symbols that alluded to a mystery, and were often understood as a sacred and effective sign. In Christian art we find abbreviations of the names of Jesus and of Christ in various forms.

Any good dictionary of symbols will describe the development and interpretation of each of the parts of the different monograms of Christ. Some of these will be relevant to the *Camino de Santiago*.

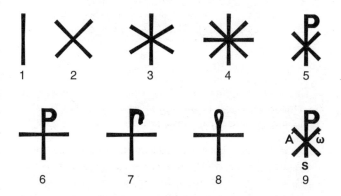

I The simple vertical bar is a Greek 'j' (pronounced like the Latin 'i': 'iota'), the first letter of 'Jesus' – that is, 'Iesus'. Such signs are more than mere letters. The vertical bar also suggests man who rises up, the faith that is directed to God so as to receive what comes from on high. The same bar can also designate the downward movement of the grace of God.

*The 'chi-rho' sign and a star on the portal of
the church of San Román, Cirauqui.*

2 The large 'X' is the Greek 'chi' (similar to the hoarse 'h'
   sound common in Spanish); in Latin, 'ch', almost a 'k'.
   Meaning emerges from the pronunciation: 'christus' or
   'Christ'.

3 If the two are united, the iota and the chi, not only is the
   name 'Jesus' linked with the title 'Christ' in a simple monogram, but the sign now takes on new allusions: the star
   symbol of the Three Wise Men, the wheel (with six radiating spokes) and the rose window – see the monogram from
   the portal of the church of San Román in Cirauqui, ignor-
   ing the rest of the letters.

4 If we superimpose a cross upon the Greek 'chi', we have
   the venerable symbol of the wheel with eight spokes, which
   since antiquity has been interpreted as signifying birth and
   death, or death and life in an eternal rotation. We also find
   this relationship – leaving aside the other letters – in the

doorway of the Plaza de las Platerías of the cathedral of Santiago. It is no accident that we are presented here with the symbol of the eternal rotation of death and life. Santiago is in the west. This is the direction in which the sun sets and dies. The sun's course – rising in the east, signifying life during the day, and setting in the west – shows us this every day. After birth, man only encounters his way in life when he accepts death. None the less, for Christians the onward trek westward is at the same time the preparation for a new life in Christ. This thought is developed symbolically on the Way of St James by other 'abbreviations of letters'.

5 In this image the two Greek letters *chi* and *rho* that begin the title 'Christ' are presented together and united. This symbol refers to Christ, as does the variation shown as (6), in which a cross is united with 'rho'. There are those, however, who interpret this last symbol and the essential basic structure of the *chi-rho* as a Christian modification of the *ankh*, which was a symbol of life in the Egyptian religions. An example of this is the simplified *chi-rho* (8) found in the Mozarabic monastery of San Miguel de Escalada.

6 These simple uses of the *chi-rho* looked at so far receive a further elaboration in the two Greek letters (A) or *Alpha*, 'the beginning', and (Ω) *Omega*, 'the end', which are hung from the 'chi', and the Latin letter 'S' for *soter* in Greek, *Salvator* in Latin, 'Saviour', hung from the vertical bar of the Greek *iota* of some examples. Revelation 1.8 records the phrase, 'I am Alpha and Omega, the beginning and the ending', and the whole symbol can be taken to stand for Christ, the Saviour of mankind and the beginning and the end.

There are other forms and variations of monograms for the name of Christ, but the outline presented here is sufficient to enable you to recognize the specific form of the *chi-rho* as a sign present on the Way of St James. The idea of the road from earthly life to death, from east to west according to the path traced daily by the sun, has been dealt with. The oldest sign for the sun is a circle surrounding a cross, to which was later

27

added an 'X'. The sun is for many peoples the centre and origin of the cosmos, a revelation of the divine. This, the source of light, is immortal, given that it rises in the morning, follows its course across the sky and sinks every evening into the realm of the dead, only to rise again the next day. The *chi-rho* recalls the wheel of the sun, and in relation with the sign of Christ has become the symbol of he who was 'the dayspring from on high' (Luke 1.78). The comparison of Christ with the sun was already known in the third century. Christ came to occupy the place that in the ancient world was occupied by the sun-god Apollo or the Roman Emperor. Just as the sun rises, follows its course, gives life and is hidden, only to rise once more, so Christ came into the world to show mankind the way to the Father and free us from the power of death.

On the Way of St James the route is enacted from east to west, from the beginning to the end. The altered position of the 'A' and the 'O' in the *chi-rho* indicates this. Normally one writes from left to right. On the Way of St James we also find the letters placed right (A) to left (O): that is, we walk with the sun (Christ) from east to west, from the beginning to the end, from sunrise to sunset. Christ is the companion who shares our journey to the tomb of the Apostle St James, who accompanied and lived with the Lord for a time during his earthly pilgrimage, when 'his face did shine as the sun' (Matt. 17.2). This path of pilgrimage physically marked out in the form of the Way of St James is only a symbol of life, of one's whole existence. The true path of pilgrimage is the course of each person's life.

In the graphic representation of the monograms on the Way of St James we are presented in symbolic form with the faith of the pilgrims and those living along the *Camino*. Christ, the sun, rules over day and night, time and eternity. He accompanies mankind on the way from east to west, life to death, and even beyond death, to resurrection and the eternal Kingdom of the Father.

Part 4
Heart's Desire – the Star Points the Way

THE ROUTE

From Puente la Reina to Logroño

➡ Puente la Reina/Gares: a metal statue of St James marks the point where the road from Ibañeta and the one from Somport unite to form the *Camino Francés*: 'And from there they form one sole road all the way to Santiago', the *Codex Calixtinus* tells us. The bridge over the river Arga, built by Doña Mayor (or Urraca), the wife of Sancho III 'el Mayor' (1000–35) and/or Doña Estefania, the wife of Garcíia de Nájera, give the locality its name. In this period, and for a variety of military, economic and political reasons, the *Camino* ran from Pamplona to the river Ebro, continuing on from there to Burgos. The church of Santa María de la Vega or de las Huertas, dating from 1142, bears witness to the assistance given to pilgrims by the Templars and carried on, after their suppression in the fourteenth century, by the Order of St John. In the left nave is the Y-shaped cross and figure of Christ (fourteenth century) carried here from Germany by a pilgrim; the hospital and monastery named after *El Santo Crucifijado* date from 1443. The town grew up around the Way of St James and extended along it. Proceeding along the main street, or *calle mayor*, one passes the church of Santiago with its twelfth-century doorway. Inside stand figures of Santiago and San Bartolomeo, both fourteenth century, and an eighteenth-century altarpiece.

29

An ancient bridge at Cirauqui.

Next door stands the church of San Pedro, with its image of the Virgin of Puy or *del txori* (of the bird). The street opens onto the six-arched bridge over the river Arga noted above.

➡ Cirauqui/Zirauki: a town on a hilltop with the church of San Román; it has a thirteenth-century doorway surmounted by the *chi-rho* symbol and a star. There are also the remains of the ancient Roman road and a ruined bridge.

➡ The Way continues through the abandoned village of Urbe and passes the bridge over the river Salado, known for the unfortunate experiences with the locals recorded by the author of the *Codex Calixtinus*. It carries on to Lorca, with a Romanesque church of San Salvador (twelfth century), a dependency of Roncesvalles, later remodelled. By way of a Romanesque bridge over the river Iranzu the route reaches Villatuerta and, shortly thereafter, Estella.

➡ Estella/Lizarra: from the Latin *stella*, which means the same as the original Basque name, Izara (*izar* = star), affirmed by the shield of the city (over time the word altered to Lizarra (*lizar* = ash tree). A popular saying with a certain historical truth to it called it 'the Toledo of the North'. Sancho III 'el Mayor' extended the road from Pamplona to Logroño, and in 1090 Sancho Ramírez founded the city on the river Ega as a *burgo franco* or French settlement. Here we find four French churches: San Pedro de la Rúa, of Romanesque origin, with doorway and cloister showing images of the Three Kings; above the tunnel are the remains of the ancient castle and fortress; by the staircase to the church stands the palace of the kings of Navarre (twelfth century), with a capital showing the battle between Roland and the giant Ferragut. Santa María del Puy, with a thirteenth-century Virgin; San Miguel, with its twelfth-century sculptures and doorway; Santa María de Rocamadour (veneration to her dates from the twelfth century and the statue of her here is only slightly later). Other monuments include the rebuilt 'bridge of the Gaol', the church of Santo Sepulcro (twelfth century, with a fourteenth-century facade) and the monastery of Santo Domingo. In the outskirts, in the direction of Logroño, stands the monastery of Nuestra Señora la Real de Irache, which was begun in 958. In 1054 García de Nájera endowed it with a hospital, following the example of his father in founding Estella. The Romanesque church dates from the twelfth and thirteenth centuries; following its extension in the eighteenth century it housed a university.

➤ The route carries on through Villamayor de Monjardín at the foot of the castle of San Esteban, of Roman origin; it was conquered by Sancho Garcés (905–25), who was buried here. This was a military success that was appropriated by the author of the *Chronicle of Turpin* or *Pseudo-Turpin* and attributed to Charlemagne; another capital depicts the battle of Roland and Ferragut. Continue through Urbiola, where the Knights of St John of Jerusalem had a hospital known as 'the Commandery of the Cowl'. By way of Los Arcos, which was granted a code of law by Sancho 'el Sabio' (the Wise) in 1175 and where Teobaldo III founded a hospital (thirteenth century), and passing the church of Santa María (twelfth to eighteenth centuries) the Way continues on to Sansol, which was owned by the monastery of San Zoilo in Carrión de los Condes.

➤ Torres del Rio: church of Santo Sepulcro (twelfth century), an octagonal building in the Romanesque-Mudejar style with capitals showing the deposition and the resurrection; also a

The intersecting ribs of the vaulting form a star: church of Santo Sepulcro, Torres del Río.

Romanesque figure of Christ. It seems to have belonged to the Order of the Holy Sepulchre or possibly that of St John of Jerusalem; its attribution to the Templars lacks evidence.

➡ Viana: in the village of Cuevas, through which flows the river Cornava, Sancho VII 'el Fuerte' (the Strong) built this large square in 1219 on the frontier of his kingdom with Castile. In 1423 Carlos III created the Principality of Viana, the title of the heir to the throne of Navarre. On 11 March 1507 Cesare Borgia was killed nearby; his remains were removed from their mausoleum in the eighteenth century and reburied at the entrance to the church of Santa María (thirteenth to sixteenth and eighteenth centuries), which has a cloister and a museum. See also the ruins of the church of San Pedro. Especially fine is the Plaza de los Fueros in this town, which has its walls enclosed by modern buildings. Viana has a great tradition of hospitality to pilgrims, although Aymeric Picaud (see p. xxi) had his difficulties.

➡ Before Logroño, make a detour to Laguardia/Biasteri, a guardian city built by Sancho Abarca (after 994) and given laws by Sancho 'el Sabio' in 1164; the church of San Juan, and in particular the church of Santa María de los Reyes, with a fourteenth-century doorway painted in the seventeenth century, are of interest. Nearby, over the river Ebro, is the Puente de Mantible or Mantibre, considered by many authors to be the crossing used by pilgrims before the construction of Logroño.

➔ Logroño: owes its existence to the Way of St James and the will of King Alfonso VI; the saints Domingo de la Calzada and Juan de Ortega were particularly important, constructing and rebuilding bridges over the Ebro. Thus the Way of St James, which from Pamplona was now linked with the ancient Roman route towards Burgos, León and Astorga, was laid out as Sancho III 'el Mayor' of Navarre had envisaged it. The city's monuments include the churches of San Bartholomé, with a thirteenth-century doorway; Santa María la Imperial (twelfth to sixteenth centuries); the cathedral of Santa María la Redonda (fifteenth to eighteenth centuries), the church of Santiago el Real (sixteenth and seventeenth centuries), with the enormous image of Santiago Matamoros (St James the Moor-slayer – surely it would be better if he were called 'defender of the Christian faith' and help of pilgrims). Some kilometres to the south of Logroño is Clavijo, site of the battle between Ramíro I of Asturias and the Moorish commander Abderramán II (844). The Spanish forces believed that St James intervened to ensure the victory that freed them from the tribute of the 'hundred maidens'. The *Camino* city par excellence, Logroño was shaped by jacobean and pilgrim tradition and contributed strongly to it.

STOP AND THINK ABOUT IT

'The Lord shall arise upon thee, and his glory shall be seen upon thee' (Isa. 60.2). In this biblical verse the presence of the Lord is compared to a star. The prophet Isaiah invites his hearers to go on pilgrimage to Jerusalem, the holy city. This invitation can also be applied to pilgrimage to Santiago. By coincidence, the Way of St James has been called *el Camino de las estrellas* – the route of the stars.

The star is considered as a sign of the heavenly, the infinite; as a bringer of light and orientation in darkness, it is a guide and indicator on the road. The morning star announces the new day (symbolically, the new age); the evening star, in biblical language, suggests, with the passing of the day, the end of time, and submits it to God's judgement. The symbolic terms used in the Bible to refer to stars are very varied. The meaning is epitomized in the story of the kings from the east, the Three Wise Men. It is hardly surprising that on the Way of St James, the star – for example, on doorways and arches and in the biblical scenes depicted on capitals – is repeatedly presented as a symbol of orientation and of longing (for example, at San Juan de la Peña, Estella, Villafranca del Bierzo). In our journey we want to perceive and be aware of this symbol and its meaning in biblical narrative (Matt. 2.1–12).

The Wise Men are so called because as diviners – astrologers in other words – they read the stars. In Christian tradition we know them as three wise kings. They represent the rulers of the nations and adore the true King in the child of Bethlehem. We also call them sages or magicians. They represent the alliance with God, who interpret the celestial meaning of the star and set out on their way towards an as yet unknown destination. As the Wise Men from the east they entrust themselves to God's guidance and his star. And they make a surprising discovery: what the star indicates is shown to be real on earth, although in a different way from the one they may have imagined. Call these interpreters of the stars what we will, the biblical story speaks of a deep longing on the part of mankind for greater humanity and greater closeness to God. Perhaps here is the mystery of this story on the *Camino*, of its attractiveness, of its elaboration in so many legends and its frequent appearance along the Way of St James.

The longing, the heart's desire of the Wise Men, was not fulfilled immediately. They sought and questioned, became confused, and had to make their way in a world that also to us is all too familiar. It is represented here by Herod and Jerusalem; here one man rules by calculation, shrewdness, vanity, fear, threats, insecurity, violence. He even has recourse to the sacred books for information, and hypocritically seeks the new-born king, to subject him to his own hatred. Do we too not carry within us something of Herod's nature?

But the longing for a more human world is also very much

a part of us, a life in which we can be as we really are and in which the reflection of the divine shines forth. The Wise Men found a star in the midst of darkness; their heart's desire and longing found a direction. They set off, guided by the star, and took to the road, leaving behind their safe and accustomed routines; they gave rein to their longing, they embarked on a pilgrimage through the loneliness of the desert, they exposed themselves to doubt and to the hypocrisy of Herod until they reached the spot shown them by the star. It threw light on a shadowy scene in which they recognized new life in the child that had just been born. God had united himself with human-kind and its longing for an authentic life without end.

This child, born in the darkness of the night, would live and later announce the solidarity of God with all mankind, above all with the poor and weak, the sick and the rejected of society. In his conduct, the star would shine for them also; a new way of living would be made visible to them, which the powerful of his time, clinging to Herod's imaginary world, wanted to destroy through death on the cross. None the less, the night of death would be vanquished, and Christ, the shining star of the morning, shines in the future for all those who follow him and thus experience the liberating closeness of God.

It is traditionally held that the Wise Men brought gifts: gold, frankincense and myrrh. They symbolize the Christmas message.

- Gold – the human person, as the child of God, is more precious than any earthly thing. In each one there lies this 'gold': the discovery of his or her dignity and uniqueness, freedom and responsibility.
- Frankincense – the sign of longing that reaches out and uplifts, questioning meaning; and seeks and incorporates new perspectives.
- Myrrh – symbolizing the relief of pain and affliction, of human limitations and weakness, of fear and guilt. It repre-sents remedying and overcoming one's own weaknesses and having mercy on others.

Three gifts – a triple message. God is revealed in man's dignity, in the strength of his longing and in his mercy. In this threefold symbol there already shines the message that the child would live and make known as an adult.

To the Wise Men from the east, the star showed the way; for the Apostle St James, Christ became the guiding star of his preaching. Jesus Christ, the morning star, lights our path too, so that we may find the right direction, the way and its fulfilment. We are endlessly coming across the symbol of the star on the Way of St James. It does not always conform to Christian interpretation, but perhaps we may understand it simply as a star that indicates the way, that invites us to let ourselves be guided along the *Camino* and along life's pathway, 'until the day dawn, and the day star arise in your hearts' (2 Pet. 1.19). Looking back, perhaps we can say that the time spent on the Way of St James has been 'a time of stars' on our way through life.

Pilgrims' Map

It's sharp out here; though we are not so high
now glittering stars blaze through the frosty air,
their brightness undiminished by the damp,
or dust-carrying clouds; clear as our goal,
our compass-bearing west, to Compostela.
Near enough, they seem, for me to reach them
from this concrete path that borders campsite,
encloses trees and a duck-drowsing pond;
stretch up and pull them down, burnish the silver,
set them in their twinkling constellations,
dip fingers in the pearly band that leads
the eye westering.
Its separate lights
Shimmer, merging in a milky signpost
That points us clear along St James's Way.

Jane Moreton

BETWEEN PAST AND PRESENT

The Way of St James – the Way of the Stars

For many people, the experience of the night sky spangled with stars is becoming ever rarer. Artificial light and air pollution cause the stars to appear dim. To this must be added the idea that what is important about them has to do only with horoscopes, fortune-tellers and the 'stars' of stage and screen, or that they are only of interest in scientific investigation and in relation to the planets, outer space and the like.

The person who, on a clear night, avoids artificial light, seeks out a dark corner and directs his gaze to the heavens, feels drawn by the breadth and infinity, the diversity and luminosity, the endless space and order, the grandeur and the beauty of the heavenly bodies and the firmament. Thoughts and feelings, knowledge and questioning, memories and experiences arise and intermingle. They range from simple contemplation and enjoyment to the insights of modern astronomy; from profound fascination to the admiration born of belief in the mysteries of the universe and their creator.

The theologians of the early Church already used the image of gazing at the starry sky to introduce mankind into the mysteries of the history of creation. They were drawing, then, upon an experience that was as old as humanity. The history of religion confirms to us today that contemplating the heavens has produced a religious experience, in peoples of every era that is on a similar level to a revelation. The sky is revealed as it is in reality – infinite and transcendent. It is distinct from the littleness of man and his world. Before any firm religious significance was ever attributed to the heavens, mankind had acknowledged its transcendence, power and might. He existed because it was supreme, infinite, imperishable, all-powerful.

Regarding the heavens, however, does not only activate religious experiences. From the dawn of human history the sky impressed upon humans the knowledge that they were part of the rhythms of nature and those of the cosmos. Positioned between heaven and earth, they sought order and orientation in the skies. The human tendency to fantasy discovered relationships between some of the brighter stars, and through their groupings in seeming images began to give them names (Orion, the Great Bear and so on), to attempt to interpret them (the ancient practice of divination) and to navigate by them. We might call this process something like whistling in the dark. The images, together with the ancient myths and legends, made sense of human life between heaven and earth, banished the fear of the dark and declared everyday events and surroundings to be manifestations of the gods, who had a place of worship on earth and whose heavenly home could be seen in the heavens in the pattern of the stars. According to the Babylonian creation narrative, the homes of the great gods were in the sky, and the stars were placed so as to represent them.

Such a way of looking at the world permitted humans to accept and make sense of existence, limited by and united to external powers of every kind. The psychology of inward whistling in the dark can perhaps be expressed as projection of the deepest feelings, fears and passions on to the vault of heaven and populating it with beings, images and visions so as to find psychic release and meaning in life.

Together with the order of the images and the interpretation of them, humans also observed the changing starscape, daily moving from east to west, in which was recognized a symbol of human existence and path of life: birth, maturity and death, beginning again, achieving form, waning. The appearance of the stars in the evening, their rising above the horizon and setting, as well as their 'resurrection' the following evening, awoke thoughts and ideas about the meaning of life. The fixed stars (such as the Pole star) at once revealed principles for daily living and religious belief in which humans came to trust. If they were far from home, seeking the way, or found themselves lost at sea, in adoring the infinity of the stars, configured in recognizable shapes and given sacred names, they found the 'guiding stars' for their limited existence between heaven and earth. In this way the star, since ancient times, became a symbol for the human condition of 'being on the way', the traces of which – furnished with many other interpretations – we too discover on the Way of St James.

The Symbol of the Star in the Bible

We find first in Jewish thought a clear prohibition against any veneration of the stars. Israel saw herself threatened by the star-worship of the Babylonians. Moses warned his people about the dangers of being seduced by the beauty and power of these phenomena to the point of worshipping them (Deut. 4.19). This prohibition – like that forbidding representations of the image of God – was based on Israel's experiences during the Babylonian exile, when she saw at first hand how the stars were idolized and the gods were depicted. Israel denied the stars any divine meaning and made them secondary to her faith in Yahweh. In this secondary position, and as things created by Yahweh ('Which maketh Arcturus, Orion and Pleiades', Job 9.9), the stars served as symbols in the lengthy history of Israel. In the thought and the faith of the Jews the star was an indicator of the way and a symbol of hope in times of darkness. As the prophet Isaiah (60.2) put it: 'For, behold, the darkness shall cover the earth, and gross darkness the people: but the LORD shall arise upon thee, and his glory shall be seen upon thee.' And in about AD 1200 the seer Balaam wrote (Num. 24.17): 'there shall come a Star out of Jacob, and a Sceptre shall rise out of Israel.'

This longing for the light, for the Saviour, liberator and Messiah is made clear in the New Testament by means of the star as an indicator of the way and a sign of the divine life incarnate in the child born in Bethlehem (Matt. 2.9–10). Later Christ is described as 'the daystar' that would rise in every heart (2 Pet. 1.19).

Why is the star presented as a symbol of being 'on the way' in relation to the Way of St James? Why is it called 'the way of the stars'? Why do we find the star symbolically depicted so often in the capitals, doorways and interior arches of churches? Certain traditional, legendary approaches, very likely influencing one another, may supply us with some information.

Camminus Stellarum – the Way of the Stars

In the search for answers, we encounter ancient religious and mythological depictions dating from pre-Christian times, which some dismiss as lacking substance but in which we can discern Christian traditions in the making. We are likely to find elements of one point of view mixed in with those of the other.

Prehistoric representations grew out of the religious experiences that led the peoples of that era to contemplation of the firmament and its stars. A vast field of stars opened before their gaze. On clear nights this field of stars was crossed by a band of brighter stars, a 'road' or 'way of the stars' that in Latin came to be called the *Via Lactaea*, or Milky Way. According to the German scholar Robert Plötz, the term 'way of the stars' was first mentioned in the *Book of the Gospels* of Otfried von Weissenburg, who lived from 800 until about 867, and was later united, in Book IV of the *Codex Calixtinus*, with the Way of St James and a dream experienced by Charlemagne.

The Milky Way is in fact an important part of the mythology and religious observance of many peoples. Earthly life was symbolized by the course of the stars, from their emergence in the east to their setting in the Atlantic. Daily the sun made this journey until it sank in the west in the evening. In the stars, and especially in the Milky Way, was a representation of life from birth to death. Louis Charpentier, author of a well-known book on the *Camino*, postulates – using the surviving place names on the Way of St James that incorporate the word or idea of the star, such as Estella – the existence of a prehistoric route of the stars, and concludes that in primitive times the route across the heavens came to symbolize the terrestrial one. In this way, from east to west – from one end of what would become the medieval Way of St James to the other – there arose, even at that early time, sacred places, waymarks that had a religious significance, and places of worship (for example, at Finisterre) for the veneration of the sun. According to this theory, then, the route is 'older than Christianity'. As a well-travelled route from much earlier times it lingered in collective memory as the route of the stars from east to west without any definite end, and was taken up by Christianity as the pilgrims' way to the tomb of the Apostle St James. Charpentier is confirmed in his ideas by the fact that the line of the route from east to west is not unique, since such routes also exist in England and France. The three routes have many things in common, such as their orientation towards Stone Age sanctuaries of ancient peoples. They terminate in river valleys or coves, today submerged, such as the site of Padrón on the Way of St James. All three lead to the Atlantic and follow – the case of the medieval way to Santiago, with only minor deviations – the parallels of the northern latitudes. The pilgrims' route to Compostela approximates the 42nd parallel.

Are these mere speculations and an opinion? Whatever our view, there are still questions. Where were they going, who followed the course of 'the stars on earth' or that of 'the way of the sun' from east to west? What were they looking for?

We find the legends, and the political-Christian explanation, in Book IV of the twelfth-century *Codex Calixtinus* attributed to an unknown author who has been called 'Pseudo-Turpin' by scholars. Here, Santiago de Compostela is linked with Charlemagne. St James, Christ's glorious Apostle, is said to have appeared to the Emperor in dreams and chosen him to mark out his route and to liberate his lands from the control of the Saracens or Muslim occupiers. He promised to bestow upon him 'a crown of lasting glory'. The text, paraphrased, might read as follows:

The way of the stars you saw in the sky means that you must go from here to Galicia with a great army to combat the faithless pagans, to free my road and my territory, and to visit my basilica and tomb. And in your wake all the peoples will go on pilgrimage, from sea to sea, begging pardon for their sins and proclaiming the Lord's praises, his virtues and the marvels worked by him.

This dream encounter is depicted on the tomb of Charlemagne in Aachen, begun after his canonization in 1165 and finished in about 1215. Today we know that Charlemagne did indeed visit Spain, but not Santiago de Compostela. The text of the *Pseudo-Turpin* – we need only compare how close was the date of its composition to that of the Emperor's canonization – was the result of a long controversy in various political and ecclesiastical arenas that began between 750 and 842. It continued sporadically over the centuries until Frederick I Barbarossa made use of it to bring about the canonization of Charlemagne, and – with the aim of furthering his own political ends at the same time – the primacy of the Emperor over the Pope.

Another legend uses the symbol of the stars. It tells of the discovery, in about 818, of the tomb of the Apostle by the hermit Pelayo. An angel told him that the body of the Apostle lay hidden in a certain spot. At the same time, with the help of supernatural light – a grouping of stars – the site of the forgotten tomb was miraculously revealed. Theodomir, Bishop of Iria Flavia, whose burial spot may be seen in Santiago cathedral, was told of the find. He was convinced by the strange lights and ordered a three-day fast; he gathered the faithful at the designated spot and found the tomb of St James, encased in marble. Alfonso II, King of Asturias, built a church over the tomb, and to the settlement that began to develop he gave the name *Sant Yago*, after the Apostle. Later it received the additional name of Compostela, possibly from *campus stellae* ('field of stars') or from *compostum* ('burial place').

The Star – Symbol and Signpost on the Way of St James

As a symbol of the state of being on the way, today we find stars all along the Way of St James, above all as decorative elements on doorways in the Romanesque, Gothic and Mudejar styles, where they appear as signposts, as references to a significant starscape. In the tympanum of the church of Santo

Sepolcro in Estella the sun and moon are represented as stars, to emphasize their importance along the way of the stars, past and present. We find the star on the Way of St James on capitals and doorways, for example, as the guiding star of the Three Wise Men. These wise men (or astrologers) are the biblical ancestors of pilgrims. They follow the star and find the child, the 'Saviour of the world'. We also find the star outlined by intersecting arches, as at Torres del Rio, and in the crossing in Burgos cathedral. As a result of the mingling of cultures we have here an architectural structure that is based simply on the symbol of the star, drawing the gaze of the viewer towards the essential (see the photograph of the church of Santo Sepulcro on p. 32). But we also find the star at crossroads, near and inside churches, and as often in pilgrim *albergues* (hostels) as in the *Camino*'s old and new waymarks and marker stones. Thus the star becomes a constant companion of pilgrims and those who are on the move along the Way of St James, from east to west, from the era of the Romanesque to the not always acknowledged signposts of our own age.

Part 5
Building Bridges

THE ROUTE

From Logroño to Burgos

➜ Navarrete: some ruins indicate the site of the hospital of St John of Acre (built about 1200), the doorway of which is today the main entrance of the cemetery, and on which can be distinguished Roland's legendary struggle with Ferragut. The fight is said to have taken place here, at Roland's Seat. Politically this area was settled by Alfonso VIII in 1195.

➜ Nájera: standing at the confluence of the Nájerilla river and the red mountain, its name in Arabic indicates 'a place among rocks', and it is a town with a great pilgrim tradition. Reconquered in 923 by the armies of Navarre and León, in the eleventh century, under Sancho III 'el Mayor', it became the capital of the kingdom of Navarre and acquired great prosperity with the new route of the *Camino*, to the detriment of the old northern routes. Sancho's son, García de Nájera (1035–54), found a statue of the Virgin, a sanctuary lamp and a bell in the rock (where they had been hidden during a religious persecution) and established the monastery of Santa María la Real, which today contains the cloister of the Caballeros, or Knights (Gothic and plateresque, sixteenth century), a church (fifteenth century), statues of the Virgin (twelfth and thirteenth centuries), the upper part of the tomb of Doña Blanca Garcés de Navarre (twelfth century) and a Gothic-Isabelline choir. Alfonso VI gave Santa María la Real to Cluny in 1079. It was the residence and pantheon of the kings of Navarre, Pamplona and Nájera. San Juan de Ortega built a bridge on the site of the existing one to help pilgrims across the river. The Chronicle of Nájera and the Order of the Terraza both originated here. Fernando III 'el Santo' was proclaimed king of Castile in Nájera in 1217. Nearby, at a spot unknown today, stood the monastery of Albelda, where in 950 Gotescalco, Bishop of Le Puy, asked a monk called Gómez to make him a copy of St Ildefonso's work concerning the virginity of Mary (*Libellus de Virginitate Beatae Maríae*) while he made his way to Santiago, so that he could collect it on his way back. The chronicle of this monastery still exists today.

➡ The *Camino* wends its way towards Azofra, with its pilgrim fountain, bypassing Alesanco and Cañas, and divides, reaching Santo Domingo de la Calzada by way of Hervías or Ciriñuela. Because of their historical importance, mention will be made of St Millán de la Cogolla, Suso and Yuso.

➡ Cañas: a little way off the route stands the monastery of Santa María la Real (1170), with a church and chapter house in the Cistercian Gothic style, the thirteenth-century tomb of Doña Urraca López de Haro, a sixteenth-century altarpiece and a museum. Santo Domingo de Silos (1000–73) was born here.

➡ San Millán de la Cogolla: hermit and father of Visigothic monasticism (473–574), of which we are told by San Braulio (d. 651), Bishop of Zaragoza, who was a disciple of San Isidoro. There are two monasteries. Suso (the upper one), in which the Visigothic, Mozarabic, Romanesque and Mudejar styles coexist, has a reclining statue of the saint (eleventh or twelfth century), and in the vestibule the tombs of the princes of Lara. Yuso (the lower one, dating from 1054) is later than Suso and is mainly in the Renaissance and plateresque styles. Parts of the marble caskets containing the remains of San Millán and San Felices survive. There are paintings by Juan Ricci, one depicting San Millán on horseback fighting the infidels. The first written words in the Castilian and the Basque languages, dating from before 1000, emanated from this monastery, as did the biblical commentaries known as the *Gloses Emilianenses*. Gonzalo de Berceo (1198–1246), the first poet known to have written in Castilian, was a monk here, and the monasteries belong to the village of Berceo, from which he took his name.

→ Santo Domingo de la Calzada: this town, which bears the name of its saintly founder and patron (1019–1109), came into being because of the Way of St James. It stands on the edge of the river Oja (hence the origin of the name 'Rioja'), over which our saint built a bridge in 1044, together with a church and a pilgrim hospital (1088) dedicated to the Virgin Mary and Christ the Saviour. The famous miracle of the cock and hen is commemorated by a specially built cage in the church containing a pair of live chickens. Of special mention are the Romanesque apse, the choir (sixteenth and seventeenth centuries), the altarpiece by Damián Forment (sixteenth century), the saint's tomb, and the baroque tower (eighteenth century).

→ Grañon: despite its situation on the borders of La Rioja and Castile and its ancient castle, the town retains its typical pilgrim thoroughfare and is documented in the tenth century as belonging to Count Fernán González (or perhaps to Alfonso III the Great). In 1063 the monasteries of Santo Tomé and San Miguel were given to the monastery of San Millán de la Cogolla, and in the thirteenth century the town became a dependency of Santo Domingo de la Calzada. Note the fourteenth-century church of San Juan Bautista with its altarpiece by Natuera Borgoñón and Bernal Forment (1545–56). The route carries on to Redicilla del Camino with its twelfth-century Romanesque baptismal font; then to Castildelgado, Viloria de la Rioja (the birthplace of 'St Dominic of the Causeway') and Villamayor del Rio.

→ Belorado: situated in the valley of the river Tirón, with its hermits' caves and the remains of its frontier castle, Belorado was repopulated and settled by Alfonso I 'el Batallador'. The churches of Santa María and San Pedro and the veneration of San Caprasio are its distinguishing features. Of interest is its refusal to pay the tribute known as the Voto de Santiago on the grounds that it did not belong to the king of León, Ramiro I, who lost his case in 1408. On leaving the town there is a bridge dating from the time of San Juan de Ortega. The route continues on through Tosantos, Villambistía, and Espinosa del Camino to the ruins of the church of San Felices.

→ Villafranca Montes de Oca: San Indalecio (whose remains are in the cathedral in Jaca) was one of the 'seven apostolic youths' (*los siete varones apostolicos*) traditionally associated with the evangelization of northern Spain. He was Bishop of the nearby 'Auca' (Oca) of the Romans. (The bishopric was moved to Burgos by Alfonso VI in 1075.) Leaving aside the tradition regarding San Indalecio, the first recorded Bishop was Asterio, who attended the third Council of Toledo in 589. The name Villafranca indicates that the French settled there, giving economic support to the Way. As early as the ninth century there was mention of a hospital dedicated to St James; today parts of that of San Antonio Abad and of the church of Santiago (eighteenth century) survive. On the outskirts stands the chapel of Nuestra Señora de Oca, with a Romanesque statue, and the well of San Indalecio, where he was martyred. Crowning the hill at La Pedraja, on the road, is the hermitage of Valdefuentes, all that is left of the monastery and hospital of the same name.

→ San Juan de Ortega: the spot has taken the name of its founder (1080–1163). Hermit, priest, disciple of Santo Domingo de la Calzada and builder of bridges, churches, roads and hospitals, he established a community of Augustinian canons that was replaced in the sixteenth century by one of Jeronomites. Pope Innocent II (1138) and the Emperor Alfonso VII (1142) both supported San Juan. Work on the monastery church began in 1152. The saint's mausoleum was undertaken by the constables of Castile in the fifteenth century, and Juan de Colonia and Gil de Siloé worked on it. In the crypt is a highly decorated Romanesque tomb dating from the twelfth century. Of particular note is the triple Romanesque capital depicting the Annunciation, which is illuminated by the sun on 21 March and 22 September – the dates of the equinox in spring and autumn. Queen Isabella commanded the building of a separate chapel in honour of St Nicholas of Bari in 1477. Finally, the sequestration of church property in the nineteenth century was the prelude to more than a century of neglect. The buildings are still undergoing repair.

STOP AND THINK ABOUT IT

Anyone who goes on pilgrimage encounters obstacles, comes up against limitations, needs help along the way. Going from one place to another may not be as simple as, for example, crossing the border of a country or shifting from one artistic style to another (as from Romanesque to Gothic). There are stages that bring with them, or imply, limits. The pilgrims of the Middle Ages came up against natural limits: a valley, a defile, a swampy area, a river. The pilgrim had to learn how to surmount such obstacles. In time, human ingenuity was brought to bear, and little by little wetlands were drained, the roads were consolidated and bridges were built. We are still using some of these pilgrim bridges today. For the pilgrims of past times, bridges were essential to their journeys and a symbol of their condition. What can the symbol of the bridge mean to us today? Here is a story:

Bridges Unite

One fine morning, when Time went forth again to regulate the day for humankind, it met a bridge. It stopped, looked, and asked in a friendly fashion, 'Hello, my friend, what do you do all day?' 'I only have one job to do', answered the bridge. 'I help those who may be on the way through the mountains to pass over the chasms and deep places.' 'Do you find it satisfying?' asked Time. 'For me it's the best job in the world', replied the bridge, 'because I can serve people, uniting what separates them and making the way easier for them right to the end; and I help people to accept you, Time, and to meet one another, crossing the chasms and deep places; and when I do these two things, I unite heaven and earth, and in this way I serve God.'

Built out of necessity, bridges unite banks that may be close together or far apart, pass over rushing torrents, cross chasms, shorten the route, link what is separate, make it possible to go towards another person and be on the *Camino* with others. Constructed out of humble materials, they are timeless transmitters of culture. In the daring stone arches of a bridge over a broad river, we recognize an image of our lives: in the image of crossing from one bank to the other we experience endurance, and we desire this in our personal relationships and in our relationship to God. But at the same time the arches remind us that you can cross bridges, but you also have to build them.

Building Bridges Oneself

Bridges don't grow by themselves; one has to build them. The same image serves for bridges over chasms as for bridges over contradictions or prejudices among human beings. Building bridges is necessary, it's difficult, but one can learn to do it. The Apostle St James had this experience. When Jesus sought lodging in a Samaritan town, its people refused to receive him because he was on his way to Jerusalem. On seeing this his disciples James and John said, 'Lord, wilt thou that we command fire to come down from heaven, and consume them . . . ? But he turned, and rebuked them' (Luke 9.54–55). The 'Sons of Thunder', as the two brothers were called, became angry because the Samaritans thought differently. They demanded punishment, but Jesus admonished and corrected them. Intolerance, revenge and violence had no place in his thought and action, which went so far as to include in his love those who rejected him. To build bridges between one person and another, to overcome isolation through encounter and participation, was what James, in time, had to learn in following Jesus.

The same can be said of ourselves. Bridges remind us of the strength of relationships. They always prompt us to make our way through the depths of fear, to tolerate differences, to unite what separates, to remove what impedes our advance, to overcome prejudices through openness and in so doing to discover new common possibilities. Bridges are important connections between the *Camino* and life. They are places of encounter. We need open bridges, sustained by mutual trust. The bridges on the Way of St James urge us to have courage, begin now and at every opportunity to build bridges between people.

Puentes (bridges)

Built by Romans, saints and queens
the ancient bridges
   single-arched
   multi-arched
guiding the pilgrim safely
across *Arga*, *ulzama*,
Ega, *Vena*, *Orbigo*,
are occasionally revealed to be
petrified rainbows:

in *Trinidad de Arre*
chastened by a day's
great exertion
I am counterpoised
in the centre of
the bridge's stony warmth
between coursing stream
zephyrous wind
and the basilica's assurance

leaving *Puente la Reina*
I weigh each step
towards the challenge
of the country beyond
conscious of centuries
conscious of sharp pavement
punishing my shod feet less
than the bare feet of penitents

on the *paso honroso*
a back-and-forth
promenade and conjuration
of jousting knights
and greensward dotted
with rippling tents
and pennants
condoned by a colony of storks
now as on St James's Day of 1434.

Karin Temple

BETWEEN PAST AND PRESENT

From the Camino *to the Street*

Along the whole length of the *Camino de Santiago* we find words used to refer to it that express different concepts, have historical significance or carry meanings particular to it and that are in themselves interesting. Consulting a dictionary may be helpful here.

- *Camino*: from the Latin *camminus*, which in turn has Celtic roots (note the Irish Gaelic *céimm* and the Welsh *cam*, meaning 'step'), describing trodden earth where a crossing is made, or a broad belt of land for the same purpose. It is synonymous with way, path and track. In this case, the *Camino* is the route that leads to Santiago de Compostela. The first use of the word to indicate the Way of St James occurred in a document of 1047, and at that point older terms derived from the ancient Roman road system were still being used.
- *Rúa*: from the Latin *ruga* or 'line', used to describe a way through a village or town or a paved surface for traffic. Synonymous with 'street', it is often found in the Galician language as well as in Castilian Spanish, and we will also recognize it in the French 'rue'. On the Way of St James we see the word used to indicate a route through urban areas, as in the Antigua Rúa de los Peregrinos (Ancient Pilgrims' Way) in Pamplona.

- *Calzada*: from the Latin *calceare* – to wear, or put on, shoes; to cover and protect the feet and/or the legs. The word means a broad, paved way, a thoroughfare; a surface on which one may walk wearing shoes. Additionally the word may derive from the Latin noun *calx, calcis* (*cal* in Spanish), the lime used in roadmaking. Thoroughfares traversed different kinds of terrain, such as swamps or areas that occasionally flooded. Santo Domingo de la Calzada (1019–1109) built bridges, repaired roads and raised their level in wet areas so that pilgrims could follow the route on foot without the need to remove their shoes or boots. From this activity comes the saint's name and that of his town.
- *Calle*: from the Latin *callis*, a pathway or track originally for livestock but that later came to signify a narrow way between two walls. Today it means a street between houses or walls in a town – the sense that *rúa* had in times gone by.
- *Calle de la Rúa* is an interesting duplication (literally, 'street of the street') found in León and Estella.

The Three Domingos (Dominics)

Three men who were important in this area bore this name. Two of them were especially important in the context of the Way of St James.

- Santo Domingo de la Calzada, 1019–1109: born in Viloria de la Rioja in the province of Burgos, he studied at the monasteries of Valvanera and San Millán with the aim of becoming a monk but was not considered clever enough. He persisted, adopting the life of a hermit in order to assist the pilgrims passing through the area. To make it possible for them to cross the river Oja he built a bridge in 1044. This river, originating in Valdezcaray in the Sierra de la Demanda, has given its name to the region and its wines. The saint also built a hospital and guest house where he looked after pilgrims, which today is a Parador luxury hotel. When Alfonso VI became lord of the region he gave his unconditional support to Domingo, and thus there grew up the town named for him. On the saint's death in 1109 he was buried in its cathedral church. Many miracles are attributed to him, the most famous being that of the German pilgrim boy accused of theft and hanged, whose parents, appealing to the saint to prove his innocence, found him alive on the scaffold on their return from Compostela. The judge who had ordered the boy hanged refused to believe them, declaring that such a story could no more be true than that the roasted fowls he was about to eat could rise up and fly – whereupon they did exactly that! The miracle gave rise to the refrain, in Spanish, '*Santo Domingo de la Calzada, donde canta la gallina despues de asada*' – 'St Dominic of the Causeway, where the hen clucks after being roasted'.

- Santo Domingo de Silos (1000–73): born at Cañas, La Rioja, in 1032 he entered the monastery of San Millán de la Cogolla as a novice. As prior he was forced to flee the advance of the Navarrese King García Sánchez III. On 24 January 1041, in the reign of Fernando I of Castile, he arrived at the monastery of San Sebastián in Silos and served as its abbot until his death 32 years later, on 20 December 1073. He assumed leadership of the monastery at a time of economic and spiritual decline, but presided over a renewal of its fortunes, making it the spiritual, cultural and economic centre of Castile. Since then the history of the monastery and its community has reflected the renown of Santo Domingo. From the thirteenth century onwards the place has been known definitively as the monastery of Santo Domingo de Silos, where he is venerated.

- Santo Domingo de Guzmán (1170–1221): this third 'Santo Domingo' has nothing to do with the Way of St James, although he twice went on pilgrimage to the Apostle's tomb. He was born at Caleruega in the province of Burgos, studied at Palencia and became a priest and a canon, eventually leaving the tranquillity of his chapter at Osma to proclaim the Word of God 'without money, as a wanderer and in voluntary poverty'. He founded the Order of Friars Preachers in June 1215 with the permission of the Bishop of Toulouse in France. It was approved by Pope Honorius III in 1216. Its members are popularly known as Dominicans, and there are female branches. It was inspired by the example of the apostles, not so much in structure as in being people fully consecrated to preaching the Good News. This religious order has given some great figures to the Church and the world, among them Albertus Magnus, Thomas Aquinus and Catherine of Siena.

Part 6
Being a Neighbour to Others

Burgos

➡ Burgos: capital of Castile, a region of castles built along the frontiers of the lands reconquered from the Moors. The expansion of medieval settlements in this area gave rise to Burgos, officially founded by Diego Rodríguez Porcelos in 884 on the banks of the river Arlanzón. Even today the remains of the castle that became the chief defence of the region can be seen. Burgos became a city in 920, the capital of the dukedom and kingdom of Castile in 1037 and an episcopal see in 1075, when Alfonso VI translated the former see of Oca there. It had strategic value, being situated at the point where several roads met, one of them being the Way of St James. At the height of the pilgrimage the city had 32 hospitals. It has many monuments, among them the ancient gateways of Santa María, dating from 1553, and those of San Esteban, San Martín and San Gil. There is also the cathedral of Santa María, begun by Fernando III 'el Santo' in 1221 and consecrated in 1260. Its main exterior facade, including the towers, dates from the fifteenth century and is by Juan de Colonia; the Sarmental doorway with its dividing column and the doorway of the Coronería, both thirteenth century, the sixteenth-century Pelejería doorway by Francisco de Colonia, and the dome by Juan de Vallejo, sixteenth century, are all worthy of note. Inside there is a sixteenth-century altarpiece by the La Haya brothers, and the choir is by Felipe Bygarni or Vigarni and dates from the sixteenth century. In the centre of it a wooden tomb marks the burial place of Rodrigo Diaz de Vivar ('El Cid Campeador') and his wife Jimena, under Juan de Vallejo's dome. Other features include the thirteenth-century statue known as the Christ of Burgos, the fifteenth-century chapel of the Constables ('los Condestables') by Simon de Colonia, the 'golden staircase' by Diego de Siloé (sixteenth century), the fifteenth-century chapel of Santa Ana by Gil de Siloé, the chapel of Santa Tecla, the cloister and the museum, to which has been added the chapel of Santiago. In the rest of the city, notable features include the church of San Nicolás with its altarpiece (fifteenth century) by Simon de Colonia and possibly also by his son Francisco. The churches of San Gil or San Egidio (who inspired much devotion among pilgrims and French merchants), San Lesmes (a pilgrim saint), Santa María la Real y Antigua, Santa Agueda or Gadea (where Alfonso VI was forced by El Cid to swear that he had taken no part in the death of his brother Sancho), Santa María de Gamonal and the ruins of San Juan are also of interest. The palace dating from 1482, known as the Casa del Cordón, and the sixteenth-century Casa de Miranda are both worth seeing. A little outside the city are several other monuments that will reward a visit. To the east stands the monastery of Las Huelgas, founded by Alfonso VIII in 1184 in the Cistercian Gothic style, where from the reign of Fernando III 'el Santo' onwards, various kings were crowned and knights dubbed by a singular, articulated figure of St James. To the west, the Hospital del Rey, founded by Alfonso VIII in 1195 for Cistercian monks, today houses the Law faculty of the University of Burgos. The doors of its church, by Juan de Valmaseda (sixteenth century), show a group of pilgrims and are unique. San Amaro, another pilgrim saint, is buried and venerated in the cemetery chapel. The charterhouse or *cartuja* of Miraflores was built between 1454 and 1499 by Juan and Simon de Colonia. It is the burial place or pantheon of the parents of queen Isabella 'la Católica' and other members of the royal family, and has an altarpiece by Gil de Siloé, paintings and decoration by Diego de la Cruz, a canvas of the Annunciation by Pedro Berruguete and a

Flemish-Hispanic triptych. The monastery of San Pedro de
Cardeña, one of the first Benedictine houses in Spain, is today
occupied by Trappists. About 200 monks were massacred by
the Moors, according to the Chronicle of Alfonso X, and are
commemorated in the Cloister of the Martyrs. Here too is the
chapel where El Cid was buried until his remains were moved
to Burgos cathedral in 1921.

> 'Most blessed James, light and honour of Spain, venerated
> patron, keep us in peace.'

*Inscription above the doorway of the entrance to the church of the
Hospital del Rey in Burgos.*

Stop and Think About It

The virtue of hospitality is very ancient. It applied equally
to friends and to strangers asking for shelter. The medieval
pilgrims to Santiago were also strangers and, thrown together
with the odd rascal, thief and dishonest tavern-keeper,
experienced the shelter offered by numerous monasteries,
hospitals and inns. Burgos, precisely because of the number
of places where pilgrims found accommodation, was a significant halt on its stretch of the pilgrimage route. It seems fitting,
then, that we should devote some attention to this aspect of
the *Camino*. Whether they were monasteries, hospitals, inns
or houses for pilgrims, all these institutions shared a common
dedication to neighbour, whether in the form of hospitality,
care of the sick or accompanying the dying in their last hour.
But what can 'dedication to one's neighbour' mean and be for
us today?

Who is My Neighbour?

In the Rule of St Benedict, whose Cluniac followers gave a strong impulse to the pilgrimage route, chapter 53, points 1, 2 and 15, state clearly how strangers are to be treated:

> All those who arrive at the monastery must be received as if they were Christ himself, for He once told us 'I was a stranger and you took me in'. To all must be given the honour due to them, especially to those who are united with us in the faith and to pilgrims. Very special attention must be paid to the welcome extended to the poor and to pilgrims.

Hospitality is more than supplying food and drink. It means a total dedication to our neighbour. The Benedictine vision of Christ – and this is also true of all the religious communities along the *Camino de Santiago* – is the fundamental reason for dedication to neighbour, to his or her bodily well-being and the salvation of souls. In León, in the Palace of the Guzmán family, we find a painting in which St Augustine washes the feet of a pilgrim and in him sees Christ.

We know how difficult it is to act this way today, faced with a growing atmosphere of selfishness. In every situation of our lives we are presented anew with the question: 'Who is my neighbour?' It's the same question with which a Pharisee sought to provoke Jesus. He answered him with the parable of the Good Samaritan (Luke 10.25–37). A man fell among thieves. A priest and a Levite of the Temple passed by, saw him and continued on their way. A Samaritan also came along; he saw the man, helped him and entrusted him to the care of the next inn, paying his expenses. Finally Jesus asked the Pharisee, 'Which now of these three . . . was neighbour unto him that fell among the thieves?' The answer came quickly – almost too quickly to notice that Jesus had altered the perspective of the original question. There is more to it now than the answer to the question: 'Who is my neighbour?' Rather, it is between me and the question: 'How can I make myself a neighbour to someone else?'

Being and Becoming a Neighbour to Someone Else

Who is my neighbour? This question seeks standards of conduct, rules and moral principles. Perhaps it also seeks institutions that will take responsibility, and justifications for my usual way of behaving. How can I make myself a neighbour to others? This question touches me, rouses me to action. There are no rules. Perhaps I become aware that someone needs me now, and I either approach or ignore them. But whoever becomes aware of someone's need is linked to that person before God and, having seen their need, cannot then inwardly deny having seen it. The process of making oneself a neighbour to others begins in normal daily life. When I take time for the person who needs me at a given moment, I approach, listen to, remain in conversation with, learn from, support, share with, go part of the way with that person, paying attention to their worries, caring for them . . . When I begin to be another's neighbour, that person changes and changes me and my surroundings. Then confidence is extended instead of fear, openness instead of narrowness, mutual understanding instead of reciprocal distrust. We will be neighbours, close to one another.

To be a neighbour to the pilgrim implies more than providing him with a place to sleep, more than giving food to one who is hungry. It's a spiritual posture that is reflected in the observation of a German pilgrim, Christa Petri, that 'There are moments when a rose is more important than a piece of bread.'

'Go, and do thou likewise' (Luke 10.37), Jesus said on ending his dialogue with the Pharisee. We too are invited to do likewise, given that this is the way of life towards God, surpassing death. Our journey along the *Camino de Santiago* can be a practice ground, a beginning of being a neighbour.

My Friend

I pressed the hand of my friend, Lord,
And suddenly, before his sad and anxious face, I feared
Your absence in his heart.
I was embarrassed, as if before a closed tabernacle, as if
Not knowing whether you were there or not.

If you were not there, Lord, we would be divided,
For his hand on mine would be no more than flesh on flesh
And his heart for mine no more than any man's heart.
I want your Life for him as for myself,
For I want my friend to be, thanks to You, my brother.

*Anonymous poem framed on a wall in the Abbey church of
Conques, translated by Laurie Dennett*

BETWEEN PAST AND PRESENT

Hospitality

Pilgrims depend on the waymarking on the *Camino*, on the possibilities for communication and understanding, on the accommodation and assistance provided for them. Even in antiquity, hospitality towards strangers – sheltering them, providing them with food and drink and offering them protection – was a virtue that was taken seriously. The biblical commandment about brotherly love strengthened this ancient concept of hospitality, and urges: 'Let brotherly love continue. Be not forgetful to entertain strangers: for thereby some have entertained angels unawares' (Heb. 13.1–2). In chapter 11 of James Hogarth's translation of the *Pilgrim's Guide* that constitutes Book V of the *Codex Calixtinus* appear the words:

Pilgrims, whether poor or rich, returning from St James or going there must be received with charity and compassion; for whosoever receives them and gives them hospitality has for his guest not only St James but Our Lord Himself. As the Lord says in His gospel: 'He that receiveth you receiveth me' (Matt. 10.40). Many are those who have incurred the wrath of God because they would not take in the pilgrims of St James and the needy.

With the greater mobility of populations in the Middle Ages, the number of pilgrims and travellers increased. Private means were inadequate to receive and shelter so many, nor could the many Benedictine monasteries that gave hospitality to pilgrims continue to do so comfortably. This changing situation, which indicated the needs and concerns of the time as well as the differing ways of viewing the Christian message, led to organized assistance for pilgrims and care for the sick and the poor. In addition to the numerous inns and private taverns, those who took an interest in pilgrims can be classified under four headings:

- **The Church**: papal documents and episcopal decrees at diocesan level confirm the assistance given to pilgrims. Parishes and local communities, cathedrals (that of Pamplona is an example) and monasteries – especially after the Cluniac reforms were adopted in Spain – cared for pilgrims. They built guest houses, places where the sick could be attended, churches and chapels supporting the pilgrimage and, in some places, wards and hospitals for the dying, as at Eunate and Villafranca del Bierzo. Pilgrims were accompanied on their physical and spiritual journeys, the record of their visit to a place was certified in their credentials, and they were recorded in the pilgrim books at the guest houses.
- **The Great and the Good**: kings, princes, nobles, territorial authorities and local dignitaries supported and protected the pilgrimage through laws, decrees and services. They themselves erected and aided the construction of guest houses and hospitals, such as the Hospital del Rey in Burgos. They thus created – not only for the poor but for merchants, clerics and others who could afford to ride – good lodgings that brought prestige to the pilgrimage route.
- **Local associations**: there were many groups and, in particular, local confraternities that dedicated themselves to

looking after pilgrims by building hospitals and extending to them both spiritual care and fraternal assistance. From the twelfth century onwards there were also the military orders. One of these was the Templars, founded in 1129 in Jerusalem to protect Christian pilgrims to the Holy Land from danger, and especially from attack by the Saracens. Later they shifted their base to Europe and to the Way of St James, where they carried out a similar function, and built castles and fortresses such as the one at Ponferrada – until the intrigues of Philip the Fair of France led to the order's dissolution by Pope Clement V in 1329. The Knights of St John of Jerusalem at first – in the eleventh century – devoted themselves to the care of pilgrims and the sick as a religious order of the Holy Land. In the thirteenth century they converted themselves into a military order and became very active on the Way of St James, for example in Portomarín. From 1267 onwards they had a Grand Master in Europe, the better to carry out their tasks. Offshoots of this order are the Order of St John of Acre and the Order of Malta, which are well known today. The Knights of St James, founded in Cáceres in 1161 in the midst of the struggle against the Moors, viewed the protection of pilgrims as one of their most important activities. The Hospital of San Marcos in León belonged to them. Many other religious communities and confraternities looked after pilgrims at the local level in convents and monasteries, among them the Franciscans (St Francis himself made the pilgrimage to Santiago), the Order of St Lazarus, which maintained leper houses, and the Antonines (founded in 1095), who attended people suffering from St Anthony's Fire (a kind of erysipelas contracted from eating grain blighted by ergot).

- **Personal initiatives:** among those who became part of the history of the Way through personal outreach to pilgrims were saints Felicia and Guillermo at Obanos, Santo Domingo de la Calzada, San Juan de Ortega, saints Amaro and Lesmes in Burgos and saints Fructuoso and Gaucelomo in the Bierzo.

All of these groups and persons were united by the commandment to show Christian charity to others and by an interest in helping each pilgrim accomplish his or her pilgrimage to the tomb of the Apostle. The practical realization of these aims involved different means. In addition to the most essential basic services, such as guest houses and hospitals, more specialized kinds of attention arose, such as protection against bandits, care of the sick, hospices for the dying and many more. Such undertakings derived from the needs of pilgrims and the local conditions along particular stretches of the Way. In religious terms they were shaped and informed by the image of Christ held by the particular community, confraternity or other group. Some, such as the Franciscans, saw in the poor pilgrim the figure of 'Christ, a brother in need'; others saw in him 'the suffering Christ'; still others, such as the military orders, made the protection of the pilgrim their priority as 'soldiers of Christ'. All of these understood their efforts on behalf of pilgrims as a way of following and imitating Christ, and sought to practise hospitality in the deepest sense, which can be described as 'one person giving rest and respite to another, on the road to eternity'.

Part 7
Teach Me Your Ways, O Lord

THE ROUTE

From Burgos to Santo Domingo de Silos

Here one is offered the possibility of departing from the route, but without being led astray.

→ Quintanilla de las Viñas: just outside the village stands the shrine of Santa María de Lara, dating from the seventh century and one of the five best conserved Visigothic monuments in Spain.

→ San Pedro de Arlanza: here are the ruins of the ancient monastery of the same name, about which information exists from the eleventh century onwards although it was probably founded far earlier. The bodies of Fernán González and his wife were buried here until the sequestration of church property in 1835, when they were moved to Covarrubias.

→ Covarrubias: in this village, with its Roman and Visigothic remains, we find ourselves in 'the cradle of Castile'. A document dating from 938 shows that Fernán González (900–70) was Count of Castile. His son Garcí Fernández established the principality of Covarrubias, the foundational document of which survives. The existing building of the collegiate church of saints Cosmas and Damián (fifteenth century) replaced an earlier Romanesque church; it has a great number of tombs, among them those of Fernán González, his wife Sancha (hers is a third-century tomb that has been reused), and three local princesses, baroque altars and an organ of the Castilian school dating from a century before Bach. In the fifteenth- and sixteenth-century cloister lies the tomb of Christina of Norway, wife of Prince Felipe, the brother of Alfonso X 'el Sabio'. The parish museum contains the chapter house with a Mudejar ceiling, and various works of sculpture, goldsmiths' work and paintings, a sixteenth-century parish cross from Calahorra, panels by Diego de la Cruz, Pedro Berrugete and one attributed to Van Eyck, and a fifteenth-century triptych representing the Adoration of the Kings by an unknown Flemish painter.

➡ Santo Domingo de Silos: archaeological remains from the monastery of San Sebastian date from the Visigothic era, the sixth to eighth centuries. During the period of Muslim rule after 711, the monks sought various places of refuge, probably in the mountains of Cantabria. Fernán González restored the place in 954, and Almanzor destroyed it in 997. In 1041 Santo Domingo arrived to become its abbot, as described on p. 53. In 1512 the monastery was absorbed into the Benedictine Congregation of Valladolid. Construction of the existing church began in 1752, designed by Ventura Rodríguez in the neo-classical style and replacing the earlier Romanesque church; it was finished in 1790. The monastery was sequestered in 1835, the prelude to 45 desolate years. In 1880 the Congregation of Solesmes reintroduced the Benedictine rule. Notable features include the Romanesque cloister on two levels (particularly the early part dating from the time of Santo Domingo, which has reliefs in three of its corners, including the famous one showing Jesus with his disciples on the road to Emmaus), capitals, a Mudejar ceiling, a museum and a pharmacy.

El Camino

the road is a ribbon
a path a highway a valley
today bridges and stone walls
yesterday arroyo and rockslide
tomorrow a sheeptrack
   a creekbed

a lane through gardens and fields
the road is
the Milky Way
a mountain pass a cliffside
a city street a sidewalk
the aisle of a church
a cemetery
    a stairway
a tunnel
a forest trail
the road is a rosary
the road is
purgatory and paradise
in a single day
pebbles asphalt mud dust
loam manure concrete grass
wildflowers
roots
flagstones cobblestones boulders
the road is
the Road of Stars
to the House of Saint James

Karin Temple

STOP AND THINK ABOUT IT

Jesus as a Pilgrim of St James

Only the person who is on the road comes to understand that the Way is itself the point of the journey. The longer we are on the Way of St James the more we experience the reality of this. We feel it in our bodies but we also find it in the Bible stories about journeys, in the works of art and the witnesses to faith along the whole length of the *Camino*. There are places associated with the biblical message, faith and artistic creation in a way that moves and creates silence. Such a place is the cloister of the monastery of Santo Domingo de Silos, and above all else in it, the relief depicting Jesus as a pilgrim of St James. To address this unique work of art, let us do what is proposed in the following section.

See – Hear – Interpret

Let us quietly contemplate the image, either as an illustration, as below, or in reality if we are standing in front of it. What do we see?

Christ as a pilgrim instructs his followers on the 'Way' to Emmaus: monastery church cloister, Santo Domingo de Silos.

- Three figures standing together in an arch. The figure on the right is more prominent, emerging from the two-dimensional plane of the arch, in part through visual contact with the spectator.

- The figure on the left is situated at the edge of the arch and looks into the distance; he has a book in his hands and his posture suggests rigidity and indecision.
- The other figures are in motion, especially the prominent figure, extending its right foot forward like a dancer; the arm in movement indicates the way, and the head turns, inviting the other two to accompany him and go with him.
- The person immediately behind moves arm and leg in almost the same way.
- The position of the feet is worthy of note: with the exception of the right foot of the leading figure, they are all pointing in the same direction.
- The three figures wear long garments and the halos of saints. That of the right-hand figure is marked with a cross, and the figure wears a satchel with a scallop-shell on it and the straps of the satchel are also covered with shells; the shape of the hat on its head also recalls that of a shell, and the figure carries a staff, the lower part of which is broken.

The brilliant eleventh-century artist of this relief at Silos depicts the biblical history of the way, according to which two disciples – disappointed, at odds with events, sad and inwardly blind – left Jerusalem and headed for Emmaus. On the way they met Jesus risen from the dead but they did not recognize him. He accompanies them, questions them, shares their grief, explains the sacred Scripture to them, helping them towards an understanding of their own present situation. Through his going part of the way with them, sharing their lives, they acquire new hope. 'Stay with us', they say, and in the breaking of the bread their eyes are opened and they recognize Christ in the stranger. In the encounter and in being on the road with him they experienced new life. Happiness gives them energy. On the strength of the experience – 'It's true! The Lord is risen!' – they make haste to return to Jerusalem. This is the story found in Luke 24.13–35.

Taking as its point of departure the highly charged biblical account that so subtly describes the change in the interior life of both disciples, the relief takes the scene of the three on the road and unites it with being on pilgrimage on the Way of St James. It presents the process of the transformation of the disciples and the desire to open the eyes of the pilgrim to Santiago to the opportunity of a new beginning in his or her life.

Resurrection – such is the message of this image. And it takes place on the road, on the pathways of life, here on the *Camino* undertaken by pilgrims. The Risen One – although he has accomplished his mission – is at the same time the companion on the way for his followers through his love for them. He meets them and stays with them, asking, responding, explaining the Scriptures, indicating the way in which they should go.

Jesus as a pilgrim – his whole figure is in movement. Since he has risen from the dead he has vanquished the earthly force of gravity, while the disciples, still uncertain, carry on putting one foot after the other since 'their eyes were clouded' (Luke 24.16). But the longer they are physically on the road, the more they are internally drawn to their companion.

The external gestures of both disciples express their state of soul. The one on the left is reserved, his gaze is unfixed, he clutches the book. He is decided but he has not yet allowed himself to be carried away by the movement of his companion, by his insistence in pressing forward, his emergence from the protective architectural arch, his advance into the future. He doesn't yet trust the 'road' although his feet are aligned with it. The other disciple shows more confidence. His arm, legs and body are completely aligned with the stance of the figure ahead of him. His eyes look in fascination at the face of the other. He drinks in the encouraging words that urge him to go forth, to become a pilgrim. His whole bodily posture could also express that moment when both – having physically reached Emmaus, and after inwardly tracing the way leading from disillusion to growing trust – beg their companion 'Stay with us' (Luke 24.29).

The shell, the satchel and the staff indentify Jesus as a pilgrim companion who invites us to walk with him – here and now, on the Way of St James and on the road of life. To the person who enters deeply into this consideration, the same thing may occur as happened to the disciples on the road to Emmaus: our eyes are opened because we recognize Christ in our pilgrim companion on the *Camino* and in everyday life.

Claustro

Pairs of dazzling columns
dance to celestial music
around the century cypress
gladdening the gaze by
an occasional figure of four
or a debonair twist.

Paving stones spell
Domus Dei Portus Caeli –
House of God
and Gate of Heaven.
I never thought
one could enter dancing.

Karin Temple

BETWEEN PAST AND PRESENT

The Cloister of Silos Speaks to Us

All along the Way of St James we are repeatedly moved to admire cloisters, of which there are large and small, Romanesque and Gothic, simple and overpowering. Generally speaking the cloister is one of the essential physical characteristics of a monastery, and some have made their respective monasteries famous. That of Santo Domingo de Silos is a good example, and we refer to it again here as a model. In the rule of St Benedict we find no description of how the cloister should be, though we do find those relating to the oratory, the refectory and the kitchen garden. The word 'cloister' comes from the Latin *claustrum*, an enclosed space, and the verb *claudere*, to close, indicating the area set apart from where the monks actually lived; everything had to be arranged in such a way that 'everything necessary might be found within the walls of the monastery' (*Rule of St Benedict*, 4,78; 66,6). The cloister is the enclosed space within the monastery intended for withdrawal. Its position places it in the middle of the monastic complex, and its decoration indicates a central function; it thus forms a sustaining part of the communication of monastic life, and in this sense it is the heart of the monastery. In a certain sense the cloister unites and encloses the four sides that mark the access points of pathways from the outside world that meet in it; its tent-like roof is the arch of heaven; in its centre is a fountain (the water of life) and a tree or column. At the same time it is the domain of the hope that unites the material world and the heavenly Jerusalem.

In addition there inevitably come to mind the lines of the Spanish poet Gerardo Diego in the famous sonnet he dedicated specifically to the cypress tree of the cloister of Silos, in *Versos Humanos* (Human Verses) published in 1925, a translation of which might read:

The Cypress of Silos

Upright fount of shadow and dream
That prods the sky with your lance.
Jet-like, nearly reaching the stars,
Casting yourself upwards in mad eagerness.

Spar of solitude, isolated marvel;
Arrow of faith, cry of hope.
Today there came to you, banks of the Arlanza,
The pilgrim of fortune, my rudderless soul.

When I saw you, peerless, tender, standing tall,
How I longed to lose myself
And ascend like you, changed to glassy shards,

like you, dark tower of jagged edges,
a kind of vertical delirium,
silent cypress in the fervour of Silos.

Translated by Laurie Dennett

The Meaning of the Cloister

According to the plan of the monastery of St Gall in Switzerland, built about 800, the ideal shape of the cloister was square, and it should lie on the south side of the church. This varied according to the geographical situation of the place, the style of the period or the respective monastic community's understanding. However, even today there prevail different and important aspects of the cloister that are essential for monastic life.

- In the first place, the cloister unites the dependent parts of the monastery: chapter house, library, refectory, dormitory, work and communal spaces. Before the eighth century these dependencies – as today can still be seen in Carthusian houses – were grouped around the porch or entrance to the monastery. The cloister was the co-ordinating factor in the rhythm of daily life, the link between the Benedictine *ora* (prayer) and *labora* (work), between meals and sleep, between solitude and life in community. In Silos the cloister has two storeys, which is infrequent, but undoubtedly the surrounding buildings were originally intended to be of double height as well.

- The cloister was used as a meeting place and as one of *statio* or recollection. As a meeting place it promoted communication – the discussion of the affairs of the community and the expression of opinion. Later on chapter houses came into being, assuming these functions and adding new ones. But today the cloister is still the place of recollection, for the individual and for the community. At a given moment the monks leave their activities and gather in the cloister for a period of *statio*, each leaving aside external things and gathering himself into his own interior space before all go into the church together for prayer in the choir.

- Cloisters invite one to silence and a slow pace. To complete a round of the quadrangle beneath the arches and still be in the open air offers a new perspective through immersion in interior space; it changes the way we see light and shadow. Walking round and round in this simulacrum of our earthly pilgrimage leads to the contemplation of our own existence and moves us to change. The artistic decoration of many cloisters supported and motivated the monks in their struggle for improvement. Romanesque cloisters from the eleventh century onwards were particularly strong on narrative. The columns and capitals, the bases and reliefs are carved and adorned with biblical and profane motifs. Viewers are drawn to them, awestruck with admiration. The sculptures portray earth and heaven, last things and salvation, the past and the eternal, scenes from daily life and the celestial Jerusalem, and move those who see them to contemplative prayer.

The Message of the Cloister

Santo Domingo de Silos, the famous monastery that stands a little way off the *Camino de Santiago*, gives a modest impression from the outside. A completely different world opens on passing through the side entrance of the Romanesque cloister. If we are lucky enough to be there at an uncrowded time we will be captivated by the two-storey arrangement, the silence and the harmony, the tall cypress and the fountain in the centre. Coming in from outside we will experience, at least for a few minutes, a place of peace that the many visitors, the voices of the guides and the photographers change into a buzzing hive. None the less this falls away when, curious and moved to silence, we allow ourselves to be enchanted by the architectural composition, the capitals with their fabulous creatures, birds, decorations and biblical motifs on the different pairs of columns, as on the Mudejar coffered ceiling with the most varied scenes of late fourteenth-century life.

All this is surpassed by the six reliefs by the so-called first Master, an artist of genius whose work is highly detailed and very personal and whose subject is the message of the new life in Christ. In three of the corners there are two reliefs arranged according to themes: the Descent from the Cross, the Entombment and the Resurrection; Christ as a pilgrim to Santiago with the disciples on the way to Emmaus, and the appearance to the disciples and an incredulous Thomas; the Ascension and Pentecost. The intensity of expression in these reliefs is bound to affect any viewer deeply. The clear and simple outlines induce a peace that invites inward thought.

Two other reliefs by the so-called second Master (twelfth century), with the themes of the Tree of Jesse and the Annunciation, complete the scheme of the four corners of this cloister. This *claustrum* or enclosed space makes it possible for us to understand the cloister itself and the monastery as a whole. In the midst of the diversity of the world we encounter a space of unity and peace. From the noise of the motorway we enter a place of silence, and we are invited to contemplate the message sculpted in the stone of Silos. In the 'picture book' of the reliefs and capitals our gaze is held by the biblical message interpreted by an anonymous artist. The stone images invite us to regard and address them. Looked at in this way, after a time they begin to speak. They tell of the action of God in history, of his gift to humankind in Jesus of Nazareth, of sin and forgiveness, of oppression and liberation. They announce Jesus the Christ, the Saviour of the world, the Lord of heaven and earth until the end of time. They are at once homilies in stone and acts of praise that also remind, exhort, teach and encourage the modern admirer.

The Star over the Field

It's like getting ready for any birth,
the womb of familiarity
that enclosed comfort
cocooned vague sleep of the known world,
yet
sensing a crack of light
or maybe a star that

beckons inspires draws
towards an inevitable
new unconceived-of life,
a misty ancestral memory,
the yearning of seed in the soil
nourished by the compost of a life,
already inhabited, half-awake.

Whether entering or leaving the road of stars,
that splash of milk across the heavens
which also lies stretched over the land,
is probably not even considered
as it is trod by feeling souls
on their journey to unknown rebirth.

Colin Hudson

Part 8
Withstanding Times of Desolation

THE ROUTE

From Burgos to León

Leaving Burgos by the Malatos bridge and passing the Hospital del Rey, the *Camino* carries on along the river Arlanzón, which has now absorbed the river Ubierna, only to pass it in the outskirts of Tardajos and continue through the area of Urel (at times very wet underfoot) and on to Rabé de las Calzadas and Hornillos del Camino, villages with an ancient and valuable tradition of hospitality. The *meseta*, the arid plain of Old Castile, makes a strong impression as the route passes close to the hermitage of San Boal or Baudilio (Sambol). In Roman times, certain places in this region had a certain military importance, such as Tardajos (Augustobriga) and Rabé de las Calzadas (on the Cluniac road to Juliobriga, near Reinosa, and linked by the *Camino Francés* to the route from Astorga to Bordeaux and/or Tarragona). Nearby is Sasamón, the military headquarters of Caesar Augustus who, in the struggle against the northern tribes, was trying to secure access to the sea so as to dominate the *meseta* to the north of Burgos, the Upper Ebro and the northern slopes. Even today one can see Roman remains in the church of Santa María la Real in Sasamón, which has a rich and lively history; here are the precious remains of earlier eras, among them a cloister and a plateresque altar dedicated to St James. Even the Napoleonic period has left its mark.

➡️ The route continues through Hontanas, with its tradition of hospitality and so called for its springs (of which there are few on the *meseta*), eventually arriving at Castrojeríz.

➡️ Monastery of San Antón: a fifteenth-century building now in ruins, it was founded in 1146 by monks of the order known as the Antonines so that they could take care of those afflicted by St Anthony's Fire, which as noted in Part 6 is an illness produced by ergot-blighted grain; in times of hardship this found its way into bread. The disease was characterized by burning pain at the nerve ends and skin eruptions caused by poor circulation in the extremities. A similar illness called the Red Evil affected pigs, which is why St Anthony Abbot is usually depicted with a pig. Secale cornutum was a medicine fabricated here, and was reputed to stop bleeding. St Anthony lived in the Egyptian Thebaid, or desert settlement of anchorites, in the third and fourth centuries; his remains were moved to Constantinople in 1095. The French nobleman Guérin founded the religious order already mentioned, which acquired great importance in medieval Europe when St Anthony's Fire and other illnesses were rife.

➡️ Castrojeríz: the town lies at the foot of its ruined castle. It was founded by the Visigothic King Sirico as *castrum Sigerici*, and appears as such in the Albeldensian Chronicle. Alfonso VII claimed it definitively for Castile in 1130. Monuments worthy of note include the collegiate church of Santa María del Manzano, built by Bereguela (mother of Fernando III 'el Santo') in 1214, with a thirteenth-century statue of the Virgin of which Alfonso X wrote in the *Cantigas de Santa Maria*, a huge collection of poetry in medieval Galician. It also has an eighteenth-century altarpiece by Rafael Mengs showing the Annunciation, and works by Carduccio and Bronzino, as well as a figure of St James as a pilgrim and defender of the faith. The church of Santo Domingo has tapestries after cartoons by Rubens, as well as a small museum. The church of San Juan, which belonged to the Knights of St John, has a fine cloister. There is also a convent of Poor Clares. There once existed a Franciscan monastery and a church of Santiago. Leaving the town, the *Camino* ascends the slopes known as the Mostelares, and descends close to the fountain named for 'el Piojo' (the louse).

➔ This leads to the bridge over the river Pisuerga: near the hermitage of San Nicolás, restored as a pilgrim hostel, stands the so-called '*puente de Itero*', or 'bridge of the Way', built by Alfonso VII; today it marks the boundary between the provinces of Burgos and Palencia. The route then enters the '*campi Gothorum*' or 'fields of the Goths' mentioned in the Albeldensian Chronicle, collectively known today as 'tierra de Campos' or 'country of the big landholdings'.

➔ Boadilla del Camino: near the sixteenth-century church of the Assumption, which has a seventeenth-century altarpiece and a transitional Gothic baptismal font, stands the fifteenth-century column, or 'rollo' – a juridical boundary marker. In the outskirts of Frómista the route crosses the Canal de Castilla, a work carried out by the Marqués de la Enseñada in the eighteenth century.

➔ Frómista: the name derives from the Latin *frumentum* or grain, though some claim that it is of Visigothic origin. The church of San Martín was founded by the wife of Sancho

Church of San Martin in Fromista.

III 'el Mayor' of Navarre, Doña Mayor, in 1035; in the twelfth century it became a dependency of the monastery of San Zoilo of Carrión de los Condes. It was the third church in Spain to be built in the Burgundian Romanesque style, and although heavily restored is a remarkably harmonious structure. Its 365 corbels are worth taking the time to examine. Inside is a statue of St James. The church of San Pedro, sixteenth century, has Romanesque and Gothic remains and paintings by Mengs and Ribera. A hermitage dedicated to St James can be seen on leaving the town.

➡ Poblacón de Campos: at the entrance to the village stands the thirteenth-century hermitage of San Miguel, and on leaving it that of Virgen del Socorro (twelfth century). The Via Francigena, or road to and from Rome, passes through this locality, which once had a hospital belonging to the Knights of St John. The *Camino* carries on through Revenga de Campos, or alternatively by way of Villovieco, and then through Villarmentero de Campos to reach 'Villasirga'.

➡ Villalcázar de Sirga: this was a Templar stronghold for the protection of pilgrims. Its full name is Villalcázar de la Sirga de Santa María la Blanca but it is popularly known as Villasirga. It has a thirteenth-century church with a massive doorway and various statues of the Virgin, among them the one referred to by Alfonso X in the *Cantigas* and known as Santa María la Blanca. The high altar is decorated with panels of the school of Pedro Berruguete. In the chapel dedicated to Santiago there is an altarpiece showing him, and there are three tombs – one is of an unknown noble but the other two hold the remains of Prince Felipe, the third son of Fernando III 'el Santo', and those of that king's second wife, Leonor Ruiz de Castro.

➡ Carrión de los Condes: on the banks of the river Carrión stands this important centre of the *campi Gothorum*, a fortress during the *Reconquista* or reconquest, the name given to the 800-year period during which Christian rulers reconquered the Iberian peninsular from the moors; its name is also linked to that of the Castilian hero Rodrigo Díaz de Vivar or El Cid. The church of Santa María del Camino (or 'de las Victorias') dates from the thirteenth century and has a splendid porch and doorway. The capitals of the facade show scenes of the Adoration of the Magi, King Herod and the tribute of the maidens, among others. The church of Santiago was built in 1160 but destroyed in 1809; it is a museum today, but the facade bears a frieze showing Christ and the apostles, and in the arches of the doorway are the medieval labours of the months. The monastery of San Zoilo, a Cordoban martyr, was founded in the eleventh century, passed to the monks of Cluny in the twelfth and acquired great importance; it has a renaissance cloister (1537) by Juan de Badajoz. Other buildings of note are the church of Nuestra Señora de Belén (patroness of the city), the convent of Santa Clara and the church of San Julián (who cared for pilgrims). In the outskirts, the *Camino* passes close to the ruins of the abbey of Benevivere.

➡ The way to Sahagún: the route passes through Quintanilla and Calzadilla de la Cueza, Santa María de las Tiendas (founded by a knight of Santiago for pilgrims), Ledigos, Terradillos de los Templarios, Moratinos and San Nicolás del Real Camino, to cross the river Valderaduey (the name derives from *aratoi*, an ancient iberian word meaning 'flatlands').

➡ Sahagún: Facundus and Primitivus, the martyred sons of the centurion San Marcelo and his wife Santa Nonia, were honoured in this city on the banks of the river Cea, and one of them gave his name to it: Sanctus Facundus, Sanfagund, Sahagún. Situated almost in the middle of nowhere and hard to defend, it was none the less an ancient waystation even in Roman times. It had a monastery in the ninth century. In 1080, thanks to Alfonso VI and his wife Constanza (the king's remains and those of his four wives are today housed in the Benedictine convent), the abbey of San Benito became the 'Spanish Cluny', reinforcing both the Reform and the *Camino de Santiago*. A charter between Alfonso VI and the merchants of the newly reconquered areas gave Sahagún its rights as a city. This locality saw a constant rising and slackening of interests and influences of every kind. Today, culturally speaking it is little more than a setting for ruins and legends. As in many other places on the jacobean way, the Napoleonic wars, the nineteenth-century sequestration of church property and various fires have left their mark. Notable monuments include: the ruins of the monastery of San Benito (eleventh and twelfth centuries, but originally dedicated to saints Facundus and Primitivus); the church of San Tirso, Romanesque and Mudejar (eleventh and twelfth centuries); the church of San Lorenzo, Gothic and Mudejar (thirteenth century); the ruins of the convent of La Peregrina (thirteenth century); the museum of the Benedictine convent, in the abbey of Santa Cruz (among its treasures are a sixteenth-century tabernacle by Enrique de Arfe and an eighteenth-century image of the Virgin Mary as a pilgrim by the Sevillian sculptress Luisa Roldán).

➡ Leaving the town, near the bridge (el puente del Canto) over the river Cea the route passes the field associated with the legend of Charlemagne's lances.

➡ The route carries on to Calzada del Coto, from which the Via Traiana (or Calzada de los Peregrinos), little travelled today, diverges to the right to pass through Calzadilla de los Hermanillos. The *Camino Francés* goes on to Bercianos del Real Camino, el Burgo Ranero (which belonged to Sahagún from 1126 and was granted its own charter by the Abbess of Gradafes in 1386) and Reliegos, where in past times three important roads came together: the *Camino*, the Via Burdaliga-Asturica Augusta (from Bordeaux to Astorga) and the Via Tarraco-Asturica Augusta (from Tarragona to Astorga).

➡ Mansilla de las Mulas: dating from Roman times, when in relation to the nearby city of Lancia it was known as mansionella or 'little house', it stands on the banks of the river Esla in the area known as 'upper Esla'. In the past it had four monasteries: Santa María de Sandoval, Santa Olaja de Eslonza, San Miguel de Escalada and Santa María de Gradafes (which Cistercian nuns still occupy, as they have since its foundation). Surrounded by its fortifying stone walls, Mansilla was a particularly important town, and there are still remains and places testifying to its profound relationship with the pilgrim-age. Among them are the gates dedicated to Santiago and to the Immaculate Conception, the churches of Santa María and of the Virgen de la Gracia. In 1181 the town was given to Benavente by Fernando II of León.

➡ The way advances towards León by way of Puente Villarente and Valdelafuente to Puente Casto, the site of a Roman camp where there was once a Jewish cemetery; after crossing the river Torío, it enters the capital of the ancient kingdom of León.

Cemetry near the Alto de Portillo, between Valdelafuente and León.

A Blessing from the Meson de Villasirga:

> *Almighty God, bless this food with your divine word, and bless all those present.*

And a greeting from its founder, the hospitable friend of all pilgrims, Pablo Payo:

> *Here I am, close by the Camino / that leads to Compostela,*
> *Here I stay, like a sentinel / in this part of Palencia.*
> *The spot where I've built my inn / will never lack bread and wine,*
> *Nor delicious and generous fare / that enlivens a happy table.*
> *Be at ease, as at home! / and in the peace the White Virgin bestows*
> *It's my humble wish / to serve you most attentively.*
> *This is the message of your friend, Pablo Payo,*
> *'el Mesonero'.*

Translated by Laurie Dennett

Stop and Think About It

Time in the desert, time of trial – the theme of our reflection recalls, in a double sense, the 'time in the desert' experienced by many pilgrims walking the Way of St James. On the one hand there is the *meseta* of Castile, bleached by sun, heat and drought so that at certain times of year it resembles a vast desert to be crossed; on the other there are the periodic times of interior 'desert' that arise on pilgrims' long journeys, sometimes out of fear of the failure of the pilgrimage as much as from the enormous longing for hope and change in their lives. This theme invites us too to reflect on our own experiences of the 'desert'.

Experiences of the Desert

'The desert is beautiful' versus 'the desert is horrible': these phrases just about sum up the experience of the desert for many people. The desert is first and foremost a place of dryness and wide horizons, of thirst and solitude. Second, it alerts us to the danger of failing strength and to unknown dangers. Third, it arouses doubts and fears about whether or not we are on the right path. Our weakness and need for guidance becomes clear. Fourth, the desert is also a space of calm and silence, of recognition and reflection, of encounter with oneself, of purification and maturing. Finally, according to the Bible it is a place where God is close, a place of meeting with God and experience of God. Let us remember the 40-year exodus made by the Israelites through the desert, and Jesus' 40-day desert fast.

Time in the Desert is a Time of Change

The desert is a physical, spiritual and emotional challenge that is presented to us. To bear up under solitude and thirst, to stick to our path across the immense open spaces, highlights our condition as pilgrims. To these challenges must be added facing up to the 'times in the desert' in our daily lives. Deserts and times in the desert contain in themselves the opportunity for change. They symbolize a situation of spiritual dryness, of solitude and search for orientation. We face ourselves, we direct our attention inwards, towards the meaning of our lives, and we seek encounter with God. In that space, face to face with ourselves and God, we can consciously take advantage of the opportunity to change. New thoughts, new modes of behaviour and new points of view arise and develop.

The desert is a symbol that awakens hope. Just as in the desert we may discover an oasis and fresh water, so also in our times in the desert of the soul we may find disturbing questions, such as: 'How have we lived up to now?', 'How shall we carry on?', 'What is the meaning of our lives, or of some concrete situation?' But times in this desert may lead us to overflowing fountains or to the discovery of other qualities we may have or other new answers about the meaning of things. These desert experiences bring impulses to change and invitations to hope that can turn spiritual aridity, isolation and lack of understanding into an interior garden, into points of meeting that are open and full of sense and meaning. This takes a bit of time. Patience is needed, and endurance on the stretches where we suffer thirst. If we allow the hope of change to inspire us, then in the desert stretches we discover the opportunities for change here and now, all along the Way of St James and in the pilgrim way of our lives.

Checks and Balances

What I don't know is why I didn't give up

When the rain fell outside Puente la Reina
And the old road ran into a red quag
Of new roadworks, so that for over a mile
I had to stop every half minute to scrape
Coagulations of sludge from my boots.

And when I got lost again and again
Between those yellow crumbling villages
Beyond the Rio Oja, and yet another
Pair of half-starved dogs, lips curled,
And snarling, came leaping and gnashing at me.

And when my own folly and bravado tempted me
To try and cram two full days' walk into one,
And the last six miles into Burgos
Were a dual carriageway, and the buffetings
From the lorries battered all the breath out of me.

But I do know, if I had, I'd have missed
A long quiet walk over the meseta,
Frost crisp underfoot, the sky an unbroken blue;
Larksong; watching my shadow slowly shorten
And edge towards the north, feeling my shoulders
Warm to the sun, and hearing the first cicada.

Neil Curry

BETWEEN PAST AND PRESENT

The Visigoths – Camino, *Faith, Art*

The Visigoths created a powerful kingdom in the turbulent
history of the Iberian peninsula, from the middle of the fifth
century until 711, when Tarik ibn Sijad and his Arab and
Berber armies overran it. We find few details, but interesting
ones, about the *Camino de Santiago* in this period.

The Long Road to Toledo

Investigation is now agreed that the Goths, a Germanic people,
formerly inhabited the Jutland peninsula in the first and second centuries; they crossed the Baltic and went inland along
the Vistula, and by the beginning of the third century were
encamped on the shores of the Black Sea.

This and other incursions in the centuries that followed led to frequent conflicts with other nations, particularly the Romans. Eventually the Goths provoked the fall of the Roman Empire. At the end of the fifth century they established the Ostrogothic kingdom under Theodoric, with its capital at Ravenna on the Adriatic coast of Italy, only to become subjects of the Byzantine empire somewhat later.

Gothic tribes under Alaric had sacked Rome in 411, and by 418 they were present in Aquitaine, Narbonne and Toulouse in southern France. They established the kingdom of Toulouse and crossed the Pyrenees, taking up arms against the Suevians in 468. They fought their way northward against the Franks (another Germanic people, whose king, Clovis, had received Christian baptism in 498 or 499), losing the battle of Vouille, near Poitiers, in 507 and moving their seat of power to Narbonne. After the destruction of the kingdom of Toulouse, and hard pressed by the Franks, the search began for a definitive capital for the Visigothic kingdom. The place chosen was Toledo, in 534.

From Arianism to Catholic Orthodoxy

After making contact with the emperor Constantine and putting themselves at his service defending the frontiers of the Roman Empire, the Goths eventually crossed the Danube in 376 in their steady course of invasion. They encountered Christianity and were converted soon after. The Arian Bishop Ulfila (311–382) had much to do with this, and translated the Scriptures into the Gothic language. The year 380 is usually cited as the point when the Goths left off paganism and were converted to Arian Christianity. From then on many of their problems stemmed from their adoption of Arianism, especially in their contacts with the Franks and the Hispanic tribes.

Arianism developed out of the preaching of the priest Arius (260–336), who was active in Alexandria and defended the doctrine that the Logos (Christ, the Son of God) was not eternal but was created by God before the beginning of time as an imperfect being capable of suffering. He was thus not equal to God the Father, the Omnipotent. Although this doctrine was condemned as heretical at the Council of Nicaea in 325, and at that of Constantinople in 381, it spread throughout the eastern part of the Empire. Their adoption of Arianism created conflict for the Goths, or Visigoths, wherever they came in contact with orthodox Catholic peoples, and it was an impediment to political unity once their kingdom was established at Toledo. It even led to wholesale persecutions, exemplified by that carried out by King Leovigildo, who provoked the uprising and martyrdom of his own son Hermenegildo in Seville and razed whole regions, among them Galicia, which was one reason why the tomb of St James remained unknown for so long. The Visigothic King Recaredo, who reigned from 586 to 601, finally convened the third Council of Toledo in 589. He himself had recently become an orthodox Catholic and announced before the assembled bishops at the Council that his whole nation was converting as well.

From Culture to Culture

The period of Visigothic splendour lasted until the beginning of the eighth century. But Visigothic art and architecture lasted much longer, and their influence can be said to have lasted until the rise of the Romanesque style in the eleventh century. In transitional Visigothic-Mozarabic buildings, elements from the earlier period (which had themselves originated in classical architecture) continued to be used: columns, pedestals, friezes, capitals, ironwork and many others. The use of the horseshoe arch was a feature of Visigothic architecture, as was the ground plan in the form of a cross for churches where earlier they might have been basilical in shape. Spain in fact possesses relatively few buildings from the Visigothic era, although there are many ruins. The greater part were destroyed by the Moorish invaders in the process of imposing their rule. In areas such as the tierra de Campos (see p. 78) it was the Cluniac reform that put paid to what remained from earlier periods. It is interesting to observe how in the church of San Tirso in Sahagún and in the entrance to that of San

Isidoro in León, with its Puerta del Perdón or 'gate of forgiveness', traces of Visigothic-Mozarabic inspiration can be seen in the arches. The ancient kingdom of León once contained the greatest number of Visigothic churches, and it is in the modern province that the most ruins are found.

Along the Way of St James we also find signs of the former Visigothic culture. Think of San Millán de la Cogolla's Suso monastery, of Santo Domingo de Silos and above all of the shrine of Santa María de Lara in Quintanilla de las Viñas (seventh century). In

Church of Santa Maria in Quintanilla de las Viñas.

the same vein we might consider San Antolín and San Juan de Baños in Palencia, capital and province respectively. In these can be clearly seen some distinctive Visigothic features: the eight-pointed cross, the lively ornamentation of the friezes, and the horseshoe arch and vault. At Quintanilla de las Viñas there is only the ground plan of the church, the apse and crossing, but they give something of an idea of Visigothic architecture.

How the horseshoe arch, so characteristic of their architecture, came to be adopted by the Visigoths is unknown. Perhaps they came across it in their wanderings and developed it themselves. Through the Mozarabs, this style of arch was transmitted to Islamic culture (think of the great

A stone window admits the light, symbolizing spiritual illumination, at San Juan de Banõs, Palencia.

Moorish-inspired arches at the church of San Miguel de Escalada, León.

mosque at Córdoba), and the Visigothic-Mozarabic Christians continued to use it until well into the tenth century, as in, for example, San Miguel de Escalada, San Millán de la Cogolla, Santiago de Peñalba and Santo Tomás de las Ollas in Ponferrada. The horseshoe arch gradually took on a form with a central peak but with no supporting column and of great elegance. Many authors consider that the geometric decoration of Visigothic friezes was easily adopted by the eclectic Moorish culture, which already contained many oriental elements. We thus find a fusion of two related artistic traditions, indicating how similar were their techniques and their later development in forms. Later, from the twelfth century onwards, it was that strand of Islamic art known as Mudejar that became an influence upon the late Gothic, as shown at Torres del Rio, Las Huelgas Reales in Burgos, the sacristy of the church of La Peregrina in Sahagún and various choirstalls in the choirs of churches and cathedrals.

In this section, in the light of some of the different cultures that have crossed the Iberian peninsula, it is well to recall the contacts among them, their early stages and struggles to survive. The *Camino de Santiago* was also a route of cultures – it still is, and always will be. Roads were the means by which news was carried, spread and learned about, the channel by which knowledge was transmitted: it was the 'media' of past times. News was carried by people. Through contacts they learned of different customs and passed on what they had learned from one culture to another. Only thus can the Christian world's rediscovery of Aristotle be explained, as well as how other thinkers such as Averroes, Avicenna and Maimonides came to exercise their influence on Christian philosophy. Such areas of knowledge as astronomy and astrology, medicine, arithmetic, pharmacy, animal husbandry, horticulture, herbalism and agriculture were enlarged by Muslim achievements that marked the subsequent development of these fields in Christian Europe right up to the seventeenth century. The eclectic culture of Islam and the translation of many texts from other cultures into Arabic, which were then consulted and studied in libraries, contributed much to human advancement. Nor should we forget the cultural contribution of the Visigoths, of which the Muslims of Spain were direct beneficiaries. By way of example, it may be worth recalling the magisterial figure of St Isidore of Seville, who sought to reunite and transmit the knowledge of the ancient world to the peoples of Europe, and the long-lasting influence of his works right through the Middle Ages and up to the nineteenth century. Similarly, many elements of culture criss-crossed Spain and Europe, fertilizing both Christian and Islamic civilizations.

Humankind develops its culture anywhere and everywhere, including the desert. One culture may give way to another, may be absorbed by another and may even disappear. Something of this kind occurred regarding the campi Gothorum mentioned in the Albeldensian Chronicle, and a further example is presented by the disappearance of the Hispano–Visigothic or Mozarabic rite of the Mass. In 538 the Roman rite was introduced into the Iberian peninsula at Braga, under its Bishop, Profituro. In the century following the Muslim occupation the area today forming Catalonia adopted the Roman practice. The monastery of Leyre did the same in 1067, San Juan de la Peña in the kingdom of Aragón in 1071, Sahagún in 1079, and Burgos, following a council, in 1080. Strange events are narrated in the Chronicle of Nájera regarding Easter Sunday, 9 April 1077, when Alfonso VI, who favoured the suppression of the local rite and the adoption of the Roman one, appealed to divine judgement: two knights, representing the two rites, faced each other in a tournament. After a lengthy combat, the knight defending the Hispanic rite won. In the face of this adverse result the king appealed to a new judgement: scriptural books from each side were thrown into a fire, the rite that would predominate being the one whose book did not burn. The Roman book was consumed, while the Hispanic one was ejected from the flames. At this point, according to the Chronicle, the king intervened and kicked the Hispanic book back into the conflagration – whereupon it burned.

With the suppression of the Mozarabic rite there disappeared the last bastion of resistance to the unifying tendency set in motion by Charlemagne, who had seen the unification of the liturgy as a step to political power. Only the rite as sung in Milan since the days of St Ambrose survived, as it does today. In Spain, Toledo was another exception. After it was conquered in 1085, Pope Gregory VII permitted the use of the Mozarabic rite in six of the city's parishes. In 1500 Cardinal Francisco Jiménez de Cisneros embarked on the restoration of the rite, which after undergoing the necessary conciliar reforms is still sung today. This account of the various rites points up the changing fortunes that characterize life itself, as well as the rise and decline of cultures.

Part 9
Full of Light

THE ROUTE

León and San Miguel de Escalada

➡ León: said to take its name from the Roman legion Legio VII Gemina, which established its headquarters in the year AD 68 at a spot where there was already a native settlement. Recovered from the Moors in the eighth century by Alfonso I, it acquired its greatest importance from 914 onwards, when Ordño II proclaimed it the capital of the kingdom of Asturias and León. Alfonso V rebuilt it after its destruction by Almanzor, and it became Alfonso VII's capital in 1135. With the formal union of the kingdoms of Castile and León in 1230, León ceded its position as capital to Burgos, in the reign of Fernando III 'el Santo'.

➡ Leaving Puente Castro and crossing the bridge over the river Torío, the *Camino* enters the city through the Puerta de Santa Ana or through the Puerta de la Moneda, and continues on to the church of Santa María del Mercado (earlier, del Camino). Following the Rúa del Franco and the Calle Renueva, it traverses the city centre to go directly to San Marcos, and crosses the river Bernesga.

➡ León has many monuments of interest to pilgrims, among them the church of San Marcelo, a Roman centurion martyred for his faith in the third century and patron of the city; there was an earlier church on this site but the present one dates from the sixteenth and seventeenth centuries and has sculptures by Gregorio Fernández.

➡ Nearby is the Plaza de las Palomas, with the ayuntamiento or town hall (sixteenth and seventeenth centuries) and the Palacio de los Guzmanes (sixteenth century), where there was once a convent of Augustinian nuns. As is shown in a relief just inside the entrance to the building, St Augustine, on washing the feet of a pilgrim, discovered that he was washing the feet of Christ himself. In front stands Antonio Gaudí's Casa de los Botines.

➡ The Real Basílica de San Isidoro (1063) is the second building in Spain to be built in the Burgundian Romanesque style. It was erected by Fernando I and Queen Sancha to house the mortal remains of St Isidore (560–636), Archbishop of Seville, on the site of an earlier church dedicated to St John the Baptist, which itself rested on the ruins of a Roman temple of Mercury. Worthy of note are the Torre del Gallo, the puerta del Cordero (by Master Esteban, who was also responsible for the Puerta de las Platerías of the cathedral in Santiago) and the Puerta del Perdón, where pilgrims too ill to go further could receive the plenary indulgence and graces attached to the pilgrimage. Of note inside are the casket containing the remains of St Isidore, the sixteenth-century altarpiece, the cloister, treasury and museum. Not to be missed is the royal pantheon, the burial place of 23 monarchs, with its extensively painted twelfth-century vaults, sometimes referred to as 'the Sistine Chapel of Romanesque art'. A historic occasion took place at the Real Basílica in 1188 with the meeting of the Cortes of the kingdom of León; this was the first known occasion when the three 'Estates' making up a European society – the nobility, the clergy and the people – met to confer.

The cathedral of Santa María la Regla is Spain's Gothic masterpiece, the *pulchra leonina* or 'beauty of León'. It is the third church on this site, once occupied by the baths of the Roman legion, then by the palace of Ordoño II and by two successive cathedrals. The present one dates from 1205 but it is from the latter part of the thirteenth century that it acquired its great fame, and it was consecrated in 1303. It is a church of immense grace and luminosity, thanks to its famous stained-glass windows. It has a magnificent doorway with a statue of St James the Apostle and another of him in the guise of a pilgrim. Inside, the altarpiece, choir, chapels of the Virgen Blanca and of Santiago, Romanesque tombs and cloister are all worthy of note; the museum is splendid.

The former pilgrim hospital of San Marcos (one of the 17 such hospitals that León once had) is today a Parador hotel. Founded in 1151 to care for pilgrims to Santiago, it passed into the hands of the order of Caballeros de Santiago (Knights of St James) in 1170, becoming its mother house in 1513 when the existing plateresque building was erected. It is decorated with motifs such as the sword-cross of the Order, the scallop-shell, the lion of St Mark and the ancient kingdom of León, and has a large statue of St James as *Matamoros*, defender of the faith; the church, with its choir, cloister, chapter house and museum is full of interest.

Besides these major monuments, the following merit attention: Santa María del Mercado and the Plaza del Grano, the convent of Santa María de Carbajal, the convent of La Concepción, the church of San Martín, the Plaza Mayor and the city walls.

Nine kilometres south-west of León stands the church of San Miguel de Escalada, part of a former monastery where Visigothic remains dating from about the seventh century have been found. The church is basilical in form and built in a Visigothic-Mozarabic style of great beauty. A founding document indicates that the complex was established at a time when the kingdom of León was being repopulated with monasteries. It mentions the patronage of Alfonso III 'el Magno' and that the new church was consecrated on 20 November 913 by one Genadio. The porch dates from 930. Later, a tower and a Romanesque chapel dedicated to San Fructuoso were added. The ceiling of the Mozarabic church is fifteenth century.

Stop and Think About It

In the cathedral of León we find the interpretation of a changing world, as the Romanesque style was passing away during the thirteenth century. The many-faceted symbolism of light, the origin of all visible beauty, was progressively acquiring more and more importance. In the shape of the sun and its trajectory from *alpha* to *omega*, as in the sign of the star, we have already encountered two symbols for light on the Way of St James. In the *pulchra leonina* (as the cathedral is called in reference to the sculpture of the Virgin in the central column of the west door), in the purity of its Gothic style as in its soaring and brightly coloured windows, there shines forth, like a further sign, light itself. It is light that guides us around this pilgrim church, which evokes the image of the 'heavenly Jerusalem' and announces to us the message of the light that has come into the world. The following story may give us food for thought.

What humankind needs

A king had two sons. When he became an old man he wished to name one of them as his successor. He gathered together the wise men of his kingdom and summoned his sons. To each he gave five pieces of silver and said, 'With this money, and before night-fall, you must fill the great audience-chamber of the palace. With what you fill it is your decision.' The wise men nodded their heads in agreement and said, 'This will show what each one can do.' The elder son went out and passed a field where workmen were cutting sugar-cane to grind in a mill. Once this was done the crushed cane was thrown to the ground, useless. The son thought, 'These useless husks would serve to fill my father's audience-chamber.' He made an agreement with the captain of the workmen and took away the loads of crushed cane to the audience-chamber, until the evening was drawing in. When he had filled it he went to his father and said, 'I have completed the task. There is no need to wait for my brother. Name me as your successor.' His father replied, 'Night has not yet fallen. I will wait.'

Soon after, the younger son arrived. He asked that the crushed sugar-cane be removed from the audience-chamber, and this was done. He then placed a candle in the centre of the audience-chamber and lit it. Its light filled the chamber, even the farthest corners. The king said, 'You will be my successor. Your brother has spent five pieces of silver to fill this chamber with useless waste. You have not needed even one piece of silver, and you have completely filled it with light. You have filled it with what people most need.'

Light for My Path

Everyone recalls situations in which 'a light has gone on'. When this happens we are moved to see a situation, an action, another person, or even ourselves, in a 'new light' and respond accordingly.

Possibly St James experienced something similar in one of his early encounters with Jesus. In the story of the calling of the Apostles, Luke (5.1–11) tells how Jesus proposes to Peter, against all the usual practices of fishing, that he row out and cast the nets again. After the miraculous draught of fishes, we read that 'he was astonished, and all that were with him, at the draught of the fishes which they had taken: And so was also James'. Marvelling and at the same time frightened, 'a light had gone on' for James. He could no longer continue to live as he had. Something had to change, and leaving everything, he followed Jesus. The text from Psalm 119, 'Thy word is a lamp unto my feet, and a light unto my path', had become a reality.

If we recall the opening of the St John's Gospel (1.1–9) we discover at once the importance of what is symbolized by 'the light' for St James and for the pilgrimage along the route that bears his name. There we read 'the Word was God . . . In him was life; and the life was the light of men. And the light shineth in darkness . . . That was the true Light, which lighteth every

Pilgrims in the Pyrenees.

Our Lady of Roncer valles, hope of pilgrims.

The octagonal church at Bunate, with its mysterious arched walkway and lantern tower.

Modern pilgrims add their memorial cairns to the Way in the vineyards of the Rioja.

Infinite variety: medieval corbels, church of San Martín, Fromista.

Dutch pilgrims on the road between León and Hospital de Orbigo.

The Way from an elevated vantage point: pilgrims in the mountains of León.

St James in pilgrims guise, church of San José, Robanal del Camino.

Scenes from the life of St James appear in this modern memorial icon at Refugio Gaucelmo, Rabanal del Camino.

Pilgrim albergues: the parish one at the Hospital de Orbigo and Refugio Gaucelmo, Rabanal del Camino.

In an arid spot, a rowan tree offers visual delight.

Fording a stream in green Galicia.

St James' body is transported to Galicia: a panel from the Goodyear notable, Cathedral Museum, Santiago de Compostela.

A tired but proud young pilgrim gains his 'compostela'.

man that cometh into the world.' At Christmas we celebrate this mystery when we affirm that God has become man, God has become our light to illuminate the pathway of the pilgrimage of our lives. He has filled the 'audience-chamber' of the world with what people need most.

Being a Light for Others

'Light made man' is at once a gift and a challenge. In St John's Gospel (8.12) Jesus says of himself, 'I am the light of the world', and in the Sermon on the Mount he exhorts his hearers to be themselves a light for others. 'Ye are the light of the world . . . Neither do men light a candle, and put it under a bushel, but on a candlestick; and it giveth light unto all that are in the house' (Matt. 5.14–15).

How can I be a light to others? This is the central question of this text and the invitation, while we are on the road on the Way of St James, to seek answers to how we can be light for others. There are numerous possibilities:

- going on pilgrimage is light
- listening is light
- supporting and helping is light
- being happy and celebrating is light
- sharing and giving is light
- praying is light.

We are invited to begin.

Night thoughts (O Cebreiro, October 2000)

If the notebook goes astray that's OK
If there's a five-pointed star on the head of the bed
Don't worry sleep well you've been well fed
If the man beside you snores, a large dog barks, both all
     night
Put your earplugs in, turn out the light, off with the phone,
     the alarm,
Remember no harm can come

If you see the lines on your hand for the first time and feel
 old
and suddenly remember you're not 23 anymore
And can do without cold showers and arguments over
 washing up
after shared meals
Remember the journey you took then to get here now,
 enjoy the hotel
and be content in your own wisdom of uncertainty
If your heart gets broken again remember it repaired before
 and will
probably heal once more
Make a mental note to remember the learning – why it was
 that you fell
into that familiar trap again
Something to do with the reconjured pleasure of a
 deep-rooted pain
injunction in childhood
If all your clothes are wet through and you have no
 protective clothing,
food, water nor hope
Feel it and enjoy the nature of existence
Remember there's a hot coffee a fat sandwich and a bath
 in a hotel
with thick linen sheets just around a corner or two
Step inside the pain walk with yourself discover your own
 rhythm not
the pushmepullyou colliding stuff of other people's
 dramaqueen scenarios
Remember what it was you were trying to forget and why
Then forget what you were trying to remember – it'll turn
 up later
Be in the present open yourself up to the mystery of God
Let – go
Be open to the possibilities
If you fall in love with the wrong guy remember you forgot
 to check
whether it was reciprocal first

The apple that's just out of reach on the other side of the
    fence tastes
sweeter in your imagination
Though maybe next time you just want to hold it
If you get your fingers burnt perhaps the pain of the touch
    of the
forbidden fruit was better than the longing or not to have
    touched or
known at all
Next time ask yourself
If the horns of a bull, or the wheels of a cart, or a herd of
    sheep, or a
large lolloping dog get in the way
Remain still and listen to the moment, wait patiently
Walk silently away, your fist gripping a weapon beneath
    your cloak
For every star that shoots, every sun that rises and sets,
    every
cloudscape formed and mysterious fruit unpicked or
    passing stranger
unknown
Has your name on, is a part and reflection of you and
    without whom
you would not exist
Resonate in rapport opened gratefully to the mystery
    experienced

Andrew Connolly

BETWEEN PAST AND PRESENT

The Message of a Gothic Cathedral

'And I John saw the holy city, new Jerusalem, coming down
from God out of heaven' (Rev. 21.2). For many centuries this
vision determined the designs, layouts and construction of
churches. This guiding image altered according to the prevail-
ing social, political and religious outlook. Each age, according
to its understanding and technical abilities, built churches that

embodied the idea of 'new heavens' (Isa. 65.17). Romanesque churches, for example, were conceived as fortresses. Defensively walled, they seemed like impregnable places of refuge for Christians against visible or invisible enemies, and transmitted security. The 'new heaven' in Romanesque terms was, as St Alcuin put it, 'a sublime heavenly castle', an image we also find in various configurations along the Way of St James. The place where these aspects are most prominent is in the fortified church of San Juan, today San Nicolás, in Portomarín.

The Gothic style, which during some 400 years developed many aspects and forms, arose from the vision of a world in a state of flux. Until now, the world had been viewed, for better or worse, as subject to supernatural powers. Time, the movements of the stars, the processes of nature, the abundance or scarcity of the harvest or the success of some domestic matter, could only be comprehended in religious terms. Everything could be explained as a blessing or a punishment. From the twelfth century onwards people began to regard nature, the course of things and God himself in a new way. The cycles of nature were observed, and their regularity induced the sense that they could be rationally explained. We can cite Anselm of Canterbury's attempts to prove the existence of God independently of the Bible, or the revival of ancient science drawn from the works of Aristotle and interpreted by St Thomas Aquinas. Scholasticism as a method of teaching, derived from the successive phases of logical thinking in which arguments were mustered, their basic tenets considered logically, then interpreted and systematized, opened a channel to scientific enquiry and provided a base for the philosophical and theological knowledge of the time. This willingness to defend the truth and spirit of realism was absorbed by an increasingly confident and self-aware middle class. All these elements contributed to the social background that made the building of a Gothic cathedral possible, in which could be seen and felt the expression of the human thought and capability of the age. There was also a strong strand of mysticism, particularly during the fourteenth century. Finally, the pilgrimage itself added something of its own, without which neither the Romanesque nor the Gothic of these regions could have come about. The Gothic presents us with some architectural elements that, being drawn from the Romanesque, were taken up and given new expression by the Cistercian order. Architectural elements such as the ogive arch, rib-vaulting and flying buttresses, which today we label 'Gothic', brought together, clarified and expressed new ideas. The Gothic cathedral became the symbol in stone of the 'new heaven' that soared skyward, an image of the theories with which it was believed that the idea of God, the knowledge of theology and the interpretation of the world could be made visible. The origins of Gothic lie, geographically, in France, and were developed there through the centuries in various buildings heavy with symbolism – Amiens, Reims and Chartres, to cite only three. These influenced the manner in which the great cathedrals of northern Spain were built, but we also find a strong native tradition. The following plan and description of the cathedral of Santa María la Regla in León may help us to understand these structures better.

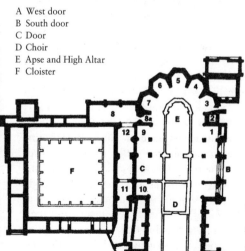

A West door
B South door
C Door
D Choir
E Apse and High Altar
F Cloister

1 Chapel of Mt Carmel
2 Chapel of Christ
3 Door to Sacristy and Oratory
4 Chapel of St Anthony (or of Consolation)
5 Chapel of the Saviour
6 Chapel of the Rosary (or of the Immaculate Conception)
7 Chapel of the Annunciation
8 Chapel of St James
8a Chapel of the 'Camino'
9 Chapel of St Teresa of Avila
10 Tomb of Bishop Martín Rodríguez
11 Chapel of St Theresa of Lisieux
12 Chapel of St Andrew

Plan of León Cathedral

101

The Cathedral as Pilgrim Church

In the cathedral of León, as in other cathedrals on the Way of St James, we find the architectural and liturgical representation of the Church as the people of God, a guiding motif that has been proclaimed through the centuries and was restated by the Second Vatican Council. The Church, as the new people of God, is something that becomes palpably real on the *Camino*. As the prologue to the Council document *Gaudium et Spes* affirms, the Christian community is made up of people who, 'United in Christ . . . are led by the Holy Spirit in their journey to the kingdom of their Father and they have welcomed the news of salvation which is meant for every man'. The act of taking to the road, in conversation with one's companions or sharing silence or meditation, is intensified on arrival at a cathedral such as that of León. This is a church to which pilgrimage is made and that invites those who pass through it to carry to its fullness in the 'new heaven' a portion of their own lives as pilgrimage to the house of God.

In the west front, with its three doors, which in León are linked by two small corridors, the pilgrim is met by the figure of Christ as judge of the world, occupying the tympanum of the central door. But contrary to the hieratic depictions of the Romanesque, here he receives as a human and brotherly judge who was also tempted, suffered and died. The last day of the world is also the first day of the 'new heaven'. The sun setting in the west is the visible sign of the end and of the new beginning. Whoever is invited to the life of heaven is subject to judgement, but is accompanied and aided by Mary, the angels and Apostles in this west door, rich in sculpture and symbols. On the left of the central door there is an eleventh-century marble column bearing the inscription *Locus Apellationis* or 'place of appeal', together with the shields of Castile and León. Behind and above, Solomon is seated on a throne as a judge – the wise judge of the Old Testament and Christ the judge in human form: before them, in this spot, royal judgement in human affairs was meted out. The common people could also present here their petitions and requests to the king, and defend themselves.

The pillar of judgement, west door, León Cathedral.

The figure of Our Lady (*Santa María la Blanca* – the original statue is in the apse, inside the cathedral) shows Mary as mother holding the child, and stands in the central column between the two doors of the central portal. As 'Mother of the Church' she looks westward towards the setting sun. Together with the Apostles at the sides of the portal, she announces her son's message of new life that confronts the approaching darkness, and as the 'new Eve', invites all to enter the gateway of the 'new heaven'.

When the pilgrim enters this cathedral with its three tall naves, he or she falls under the spell of the play of colours of the imposing windows, with a total surface area – leaving aside the three rose windows – of 1,800 square metres. Direct access and view of the high altar are blocked by the choir, dating from the fifteenth century and installed in its present situation in the seventeenth. The pilgrim must circumvent it to carry on around the cathedral, and in so doing encounters a radiating series of chapels. In each he may encounter a further witness to Jesus Christ – listening to the word of God, praying for personal intentions, making simple offerings – until eventually the pilgrim turns towards the centre of the sanctuary. There, as the Revelation of St John affirms, 'the tabernacle of God is with men, and he will dwell with them, and they shall be his people, and God himself shall be with them, and be their God' (Rev. 21.3). In many medieval cathedrals to which pilgrimage was made, the most important side-chapels were dedicated to saints from the world of the Franks, such as St

Martin of Tours and St Louis. Pilgrims from far afield found here their holy protectors, who accompanied them on their way towards the 'heavenly Jerusalem' and through whom they intensely sought contact with God.

The Plan of the Stained-Glass Windows – Creation is Revealed

The multi-coloured stained-glass panes of the 125 window openings (some 12 metres high), the 57 small and three large rose windows, offer impressive and varied plays of light according to the position of the sun. In unending progression one window and rose window after another takes on light from the sun and casts its coloured light into the church.

With regard to their themes, the representations comprise the entire history of salvation in the theological and philosophical conceptions of the period. Normally the images in the vertical windows are to be read from the bottom upwards. We thus see on the lowest level the world of plants. Hidden in it we find heads like those of human beings. Man evolved from nature: together with the biblical history of the creation, we ourselves find the 'new' and at the same time the old story or theory of the evolution of *Homo sapiens*. On the next level of the windows we find mankind in the world of his natural existence, shaped by his skills, activities, ideas and perceptions. This is represented by the heraldic shields of the nobles, towns and confraternities that had collaborated in the building of the cathedral. And above is the glory of heaven, with the saints of the Old and New Testaments in scenes from the Bible and from history: a taste of the 'heavenly Jerusalem'.

The apse of the cathedral is at its east end. The first ray of the sun to enter there illuminates the figure of Christ, the rising sun, and the sun initiates its course, later tending slightly towards the south. In the sun-lit windows of the south aisle of the cathedral (often in tones of yellow, golden and clear) we see many scenes from the New Testament. The direct light of the New Testament, which is Christ himself, makes the message of the risen Christ and the witnesses to him shine in the cathedral and in the daily lives of pilgrims. The reflection of the light, or its clarity, is what also makes apparent the work of salvation expressed in the Old Testament and represented in the north aisle of the cathedral (usually in blues and dark colours), which receives less sunlight. The words of the prologue to St John's Gospel come to life: 'And the light shineth in darkness' (John 1.5). Both sides, the Old Testament on the north side and the New Testament on the south, meet and are united in Christ, the 'sun of justice'. Meanwhile in the west-facing rose window stands the Virgin Mary and the child, surrounded by angels with trumpets. Towards that direction, towards the darkness, towards Finisterre, the sun's light is directed. Towards that direction, symbolically, we must bear this sunlight, the word of God, that is light in the darkness, so that all people may know the truth of the Good News, continuing on from the beginning of St John's Gospel. That is precisely why we find in Gothic portals the figure of Mary with Jesus in her arms, surrounded by the Apostles. She is telling us to be today's apostles.

The Central Choir in the Cathedral

In Spain we frequently find that the choir is located in the middle of a cathedral. The choir of León cathedral, with a passage through it and access to the high altar, is framed by a set of fifteenth-century walnut choirstalls that comprise a work of great artistic value. Originally the choir was a place in or near the chancel for priests or monks or persons of a certain rank. The word 'cathedral' derives from the Latin *catedra*, 'chair', while the Spanish word *seo* derives from *sede*, or 'seat'. From the *catedra* the bishop taught, as the spiritual and sacramental descendant of the Apostles, the direct witnesses of Christ. The bishop is a successor to the Apostles: he is himself an apostle, a missionary, the herald of the Christian message. Next in order are the members of the chapter of canons, a council that assists the bishop in the administration of the diocese, not only in the work of so doing, but also in prayer. The first to place the choir in the middle of the cathedral were the Cistercians. The emphasis placed upon their rule of life gradually led to the increased importance of the choir as the site where the divine office, or liturgy of the hours, was sung, and the influence of the order itself further spread this emphasis, cathedral chapters adopting the practice of chanting the divine office communally. In Spain during the sixteenth and seventeenth centuries almost all cathedrals came to have their respective choirs centrally placed. From a pastoral point of view this permitted greater closeness and more direct access to the adoration of the Blessed Sacrament and the celebration of the Eucharist (as the Council of Trent prescribed) than if the choir were situated in the chancel, between the people and the altar. In addition, the theology of the sacrifice of the Holy Mass and the priest offering it reflected aspects of Old Testament priesthood and revalued the Letter to the Hebrews. The celebrating priest acts in the name of and on behalf of mankind. This meant that those who comprised the chapter, and above all the bishop, represented the people before God, offering the victim for them and their sins.

> For every high priest taken from among men is ordained for men in things pertaining to God, that he may offer both gifts and sacrifices for sins: Who can have compassion on the ignorant, and on them that are out of the way; for that he himself also is compassed with infirmity. And by reason hereof he ought, as for the people, so also for himself, to offer for sins. And no man taketh this honour unto himself, but he that is called of God. (Heb. 5.1–4)

The bishop and his chapter, and the clergy, chosen from among the people (almost as their representatives), pray, preach and make offerings on behalf of the people in the midst of the cathedral, while the people of God surround them; they endorse, support and enact their earthly pilgrimages around the choir composed of their 'representatives'. In this additional sense the Spanish cathedral on the Way of St James has also to be understood as a pilgrim church.

Part 10

'Leave Not One Stone Upon Another'

THE ROUTE

From León to Ponferrada

→ La Virgen del Camino: this is one of the Marian sanctuaries of the province of León. Devotion here seems to derive from the translation or extension of that rendered to Santa María del Mercado or del Camino, with the appearance of visions to the shepherd Alvar Simón between 1502 and 1511; the original sanctuary dates from 1514. The present modern church, by the Dominican architect P. Coello de Portugal, was finished in 1961 and was the first time that a cement and block structure had provided housing for objects of ancient art – in this somewhat notorious case, for the baroque altarpiece. Also noteworthy are two works by José María Subirachs: the facade, a bronze scene of the Apostles at Pentecost, with St James bedecked in shells, and the doors. The route continues through Valverde del Camino and San Miguel del Camino.

→ Villadangos del Páramo: the *Camino* wends its way across the Leónese plain, or *páramo*. This town has a church dedicated to Santiago, made of humble local materials such as adobe and brick. It may be the Roman settlement of Vallata that was situated on the Via Traiana, later being called 'Viadangos'. Historians place the battle of the Órbigo, in which the Suevi fought the Alans, in the nearby fields; later (in 1111), in the same area, queen Urraca and her son Alfonso VII 'el Emperador' waged war against her ex-husband Alfonso 'el Batallador'.

→ Hospital de Órbigo: from San Martín del Camino the route continues to Puente de Órbigo, where it crosses the river of the same name en route to Hospital de Órbigo. The pilgrim hospital there belonged to the Knights of St John, and the church is dedicated to St John the Baptist. The name of Órbigo comes from the ancient iberian language and means 'place where waters mingle' – appropriately, since the rivers Luna and Omaña come together to form the river Órbigo. The historic bridge is held to date from Roman times and has 20 arches. It is associated with the battle of the Suevi against the Visigoths in 452, the struggle between Alfonso 'el Magno' and Cordoban forces in 900, and the challenge issued by the knight Suero de Quiñones in 1434 in the famous tournament of the *Paso Honroso*.

→ Geographically, once past the Órbigo the *Camino* leaves the flatlands and enters the foothills of the mountains of León, together with the motorway or royal highway to Villares de Órbigo (with its church of Santiago) and Santibáñez de Valdeiglesias, to arrive at a view of Astorga (the Roman Asturica Augusta) from the cross of Santo Toribio, and to reach it by way of San Justo de la Vega and the river Tuerto.

→ Astorga: a city with a 2,000-year history, it was an important nucleus of communications where nine Roman highways met or crossed, and an administrative and legal centre. The *Camino Francés* later overlaid the Roman route from Bordeaux, while the *Via de la Plata*, an artery that had existed since the Bronze Age, and which in Roman times linked Mérida, Braga and Lugo (and which was used by the slaves forced into the gold mines of Las Médulas), later became the *Camino Mozarabe* of pilgrims to Santiago coming from the south. Astorga's episcopal see is traditionally held to date from apostolic times. From the year 254 much is known about the activity of the diocese, through the documents of St Cyprian of Carthage. In the fourth century the Priscillian heresy was rife here. In the fifth century, St Toribio of Liébana was Bishop. The Visigothic period saw the development of monasticism,

Antonio Gaudí's episcopal palace in Astorga today houses the Museum of the Pilgrimage Route.

especially in the Bierzo; prominent saints included Fructuoso, Valerio, Genadio and Gaucelmo. Various churches and cathedrals preceded the present cathedral of Santa María, begun in 1471 and not finished until the eighteenth century. Besides the sumptuous main facade, there are treasures inside, such as the altarpiece by Gaspar Becerra and the choir (both sixteenth century), the Romanesque-Byzantine Virgin in Majesty (early twelfth century), a Virgin of the Immaculate Conception by Gregrio Fernández, fine sixteenth-century choirstalls (note the pipe-smoking card players) and a Gothic cloister. The diocesan museum is worth visiting, as is the Museo de los Caminos, situated in Gaudí's episcopal palace (on which the architect was working off and on between 1899 and 1913). Other interesting buildings in the city include the hospital of San Juan Bautista near the cathedral; the cell belonging to the 'Emparadadas', or saints who were immured, situated between the churches of Santa Marta (martyr and patroness of the city) and the chapel of San Esteban; the eleventh-century church of San Bartolomé; the city walls; the ayuntamiento or town hall, with its Maragato figures; and the ancient ergástula or Roman

109

vaults on the site of the forum, today a museum. Apparently Astorga was once second only to Burgos in the number of its pilgrim hospitals.

→ One route now continues on to Ponferrada by way of motorway and the former mountain pass known as the Puerto del Manzanal. We follow the genuine route, mentioned in the *Codex Calixtinus*, through Rabanal. Leaving Astorga we find the chapel of the Ecce Homo: inside there is a well, now covered by a stone slab, from which pilgrims used to be given water – a precious gift in times of drought.

→ Castrillo de los Polvazares: reached by going through Murias de Rechivaldo, and a little off the *Camino*, this entire village is now a National Monument. Between Astorga and Cruz de Ferro lies the 'Maregatería' or home of the Maragatos, who in the past made their living transporting goods.

→ Rabanal del Camino: today it has three churches. The parish one, Santa María, has substantial Romanesque remains, and that of San José has been recently restored to its full baroque splendour. The third awaits restoration.

A volunteer warden, or hospitalera, checks and stamps pilgrims' passports at Refugio Gaucelmo, Rabanal del Camino.

→ Foncebadón: on the slopes of Monte Irago this village is slowly coming back to life. Documents relate that in the monastery of San Salvador a council of the local Mozarabic church was held in the tenth century. San Gaucelmo dedicated himself to pilgrims here in the late eleventh and early twelfth centuries. Alfonso VI conceded the place the privilege of marking the road with stakes, which gave security to travellers and pilgrims, and in return for which the inhabitants of Foncebadón were exempted from taxes.

The Cruz de Ferro and its pile of stones: where pilgrims have symbolically shed their burdens for a thousand years.

→ Cruz de Ferro: at an altitude of 1,504 metres, this marks the point of entry to the Bierzo. It consists of a pile of stones with a tall wooden pole topped by an iron cross, first documented in the thirteenth century. Here the pilgrims place their stones, as explained in the next section.

→ The Camino continues through the ruined hamlet of Manjarín and descends to El Acebo. From it there is a view of the Valle del Silencio, the cradle of Visigothic monasticism, where San Fructuoso de Braga, a native of the Bierzo, was active in the seventh century. In Compludo, off the route in a deep valley, there is a forge operated by a water-hammer that would appear to date from Roman times. By way of Riego de Ambros the way descends to Molinaseca, with its medieval bridge over the river Meruelo, where there used to be various inns for pilgrims (a cross indicates the site of the former hospital), such as those of Santa Marina, San Lázaro and San Roque. Continuing straight on, the Camino reaches Ponferrada.

A communal meal at a pilgrim albergue.

The Gate of the Year

I said to the man who stood at the gate of the year:
Give me a light that I may travel safely into the unknown
And he replied:
*Go out into the darkness and put your hand into the hand
   of God.*
*That shall be to you better than light, and safer than a
   known way.*

*Minnie Louise Haskins, quoted by King George V
in his Christmas message, 1939*

A Prayer for an End to Violence

God of life,
Every act of violence in our world
       between myself and another
              destroys a part of your creation

Stir within my heart a renewed sense of
    reverence for all life.
Give me the vision to recognize your spirit
    in every human being,
        however they behave towards me.

Make possible the impossible by cultivating in me
    the fertile seed of healing love.
May I play my part in breaking
    the cycle of violence by realising that
        peace begins with me.

St Ethelburga's Centre for Reconciliation and Peace
London, 7 July 2005

STOP AND THINK ABOUT IT

Little by little, once past Rabanal the upward path brings us to Foncebadón and to Cruz de Ferro. Following an age-old custom, pilgrims carry a stone to toss onto the heap of them that marks the highest point on the Way of St James. But why a stone?

At the top of the pass, near a chapel dedicated to Santiago, we see a great pile of stones, a wooden pole and an iron cross. Centuries ago it was the dividing point between the Maragatería and the Bierzo. The Romans called these 'the mountains of Mercury' – the god who protected travellers and people on foot. According to pagan tradition, those who passed by had to throw a stone onto the pile. We, the pilgrims and travellers of today on the *Camino de Santiago*, come across many stones, of every shape and size. They are in the churches and other buildings, in capitals and reliefs, and they convey to us the message with which they have been charged by architects, builders and sculptors. In addition, a stone, even without any human mark, is a religious symbol. So let us each find a stone, and if we are in a group, when we reach Cruz de Ferro, let us make a circle and allow this symbol to be the subject of a little meditation.

Casting off Bad Habits: Setting the Ball – or Stone – Rolling

If stones could speak, what would they tell us? Among other things, stories of pilgrims who have passed this way; pilgrims who were tired and kept going; those who at this spot have shared their last drop of water and what remained of their bread; of conversations about hopes and fears, cares and sufferings; of assaults and robberies and of mutual love renounced; of the longing for forgiveness, of the search for God.

Our stones: are they the silent witnesses of history on the *Camino de Santiago*? Yes. But they speak of themselves and of us. Let's try and experience this through our senses. I touch and register the stone in my hand. I feel it with my fingers. I become aware of its shape, its edges and round parts, its points and sharpness. I feel its surface. My hand folds around it, it feels comfortable there, a part of me. It feels as though it has become *my* stone; is it mine? Does it form part of me? Elusive, abrasive, insensitive, cutting, pointed, lacerating?

I hold it out between both hands, I note its colour and its accumulated warmth from the sun or perhaps its pleasant coolness. It gives me heat or cold. And I? Where is there something that awaits the warmth of my self-giving? How do things go when I risk a form of life that will change me?

I look at the stone from every side; I see traces of earth and vegetation sticking to it, I see damp areas and different colours, I observe signs of abrasion and contact with other stones. All this reminds me of my oneness with nature and the changing story of my life: happiness and disappointment, strife and reconciliation, worry and hope.

I feel the weight of the stone in my hand. If I am conscious of it, I note the drag of its gravity, which can encumber and burden me, reminding me of my own useless baggage. What loads am I still carrying? Which do I want to cast off? (Fear? Anger?) Feeling, looking, taking note: as I reflect on my situation, the stone becomes all that I want to leave behind.

In silence, alone and in conversation with my stone, I make my way to the top of the pile. I consciously identify my stone with all my unnecessary baggage, and then I add it to the great heap that surrounds the base of the Cruz de Ferro. Then I wait in silence as my companions on the *Camino* do the same.

I have tossed my stone among the stones left by pilgrims over many centuries. One stone among countless stones, one burden among many other burdens. I am grateful to my stone for the impulse, for the necessary push, for what it set in motion in me, for what it has outwardly set rolling, and for the weight that with its help I have been able to put aside, cast off, cut loose – on the *Camino*.

Where a stone begins to roll, there new life develops, as in another time when the 'great stone' rolled away from the sepulchre of Jesus. Our stones, the stones of pilgrims, will last longer than we will. They will remain here when we have gone. The stones say to us: it is the same with God. All things pass away, but God is faithful and sure. He existed before us and he will exist after us. He is your companion today on the *Camino de Santiago* and every day of your life.

BETWEEN PAST AND PRESENT

Pilgrims – Possessions and Motivation

The German pilgrim song, *Wer daz elend bauen wil* (which means, 'He who would go to a far-off land') originated in the thirteenth century and became widely known. Its first few lines describe in some detail the items needed by the medieval pilgrim:

> . . . two pairs of shoes he must have,
> a bowl as well as a bottle.
> He must wear a broad hat,
> and always a cloak.
> Well covered in leather . . .
> A bag and a staff are essential . . .

These articles were not exclusive to pilgrims on the *Camino de Santiago* but we find them most closely associated with

Die Jacobs Brüder.

A medieval German woodcut depicting a pilgrim follower of St James.

them, together with the scallop-shell of St James. As such, everything had its practical application, which over time acquired a symbolic interpretation. The pilgrim's cloak and broad-brimmed hat were not just for protection from foul weather and the sun's rays, but represented the protection afforded by God. The scallop-shell identified the pilgrim and gained for that person the rights granted by the authorities of the regions passed through, but it also signified baptism and the new life open through this sacrament. Similarly, the water-gourd or bottle contained not just water but 'the living water' promised by Christ to those who believed in him. The satchel or draw-string pouch was a constant reminder of holy poverty. It also suggested the blessings to be won by humble gratitude for donations of food or money, and in turn by generous alms-giving. A sturdy staff was a defence and a support over rough ground, but it also symbolized the strength of faith, and as a third point of contact with the earth, the Trinity.

Why did so many people from almost every country in Europe go on pilgrimage to Santiago? There were many different reasons and they are often set out in pilgrim guidebooks. They are also evoked in poems such as the one below, in which modern pilgrims, on returning home, reflect on their motives:

The *Camino*

When we started, we did not know – exactly – why we
  were doing it
We had lives which were – more or less – satisfactory
We had friends known much of our lives
We had children – changed from chrysalis to butterflies
We had things: things like cars
                    things like washing machines
                    things like power drills
                    things like music
                    things like pictures
                    things like shelves full of books
                    things like money and pensions and security
We did not have one thing – and maybe that was why we
  started

When we started, we put one foot in front of the other
We still did not know – precisely – why we were doing it
The miles passed – many of them pleasantly
Our feet blistered and were slow to heal
Our ankles turned on loose stone
The rain beat its way through our clothes
The cold chilled the marrow of our bones
Some nights refuge was hard to find
Some days miles of hot dust had no fountains

When the first few of many long days had passed
We found – without words – that we no longer walked
  together
That together we spoke in our own tongues –
  And often of things we had left behind where we began
That together we shut out new experience with the wall of
  our togetherness
That alone we spoke in other tongues and of our common
  experience
That alone we were open – open with interest and curiosity
Often we met – with gladness – at the end of the day
To know our paths went on together was enough

When we got to the cathedral we sat down
We saw – through the eyes of those long before us
The blinding faith, the crucial thirst for salvation
The tower slowly closing off the sky
And we counted our blessings, several hundred of them
Starting with the kindness of ordinary people along the
way
And with the warmth of other travellers on the road
Travellers not at all like us – not in age, not in origin, not
in interests
But warm across all these distancings
And ending with the friendship and love
We had left behind where we began.

When we got to the sea at the end of the world
We sat down on the beach at sunset
We knew why we had done it
To know our lives less important than just one grain of
sand
To know that we did not need the things we had left
behind us
To know that we would nevertheless return to them
To know that we needed to be where we belonged
To know that kindness and friendship and love is all one
needs
To know that we did not – after all – have to make this
long journey to find this out
To know that – for us – it certainly helped

Piers Nicholson

The German song mentioned earlier described the stops along
the way and was a kind of guide or *vademecum* for pilgrims.
On reaching their journey's end, the 26th verse would have
been an especially welcome reminder that:

At the tomb of St James all grief and debt is forgiven,
The good Lord is benevolent to all,
From his throne on high.

Whoever gives himself in service to St James
The good Lord must repay.

And perhaps the point of the longer poem above is that through the experience of walking to Santiago the pilgrim grows in awareness of many blessings already received, and in the transforming acceptance of being loved by God that is the greatest blessing of all.

Mary, the Pilgrim

The veneration of the Virgin Mary on the *Camino* is proverbial. The Cistercians were in part responsible for this, but there is an ancient tradition and a popular devotion that unites Mary and St James. This is centred on the veneration of the Virgen del Pilar, or Virgin of the Pillar in Zaragoza, as the patroness of Spain together with St James. A thirteenth-century text relates how St James, in his mission to evangelize Spain, had enjoyed little success and was feeling discouraged. At that moment, Mary appeared to him, revived his spirits and asked him to build a church where the column upon which she had descended from heaven stood. That place was Zaragoza.

All along the Way of St James we find widely differing representations of Mary. The earliest is the Romanesque-Byzantine figure known as the Virgin in Majesty, the oldest example of which is in the cathedral of Astorga. In pursuit of authenticity the angels, crown and sheet of silver that covers the figure's shoulders and the child should be removed, since they are later additions. Mary is represented here seated on a throne, in an upright and hieratic pose; she is a spiritualized figure, gazing into the beyond in a truly majestic posture. *She* is the true throne, the seat of Wisdom who reveals to us the Christ, the word of God, the Wisdom of God. Christ, in the centre, is not represented as a child but as an adult. In her right hand Mary holds a fruit – an apple or pomegranate – signifying the new creation; with her left she majestically directs our eyes towards the son. Christ holds a book in his left hand, representing the

Good News, and his right hand is raised in the sign for witness or testimony. Usually in the Romanesque style the child is only supported or seated on the knees of his mother; he does not lean against her for any other support. Although it seems that Mary is sustaining the figure of Christ, the latter is in fact carved in the round.

In the late Romanesque and early Gothic styles, the child came to be placed in the curve of his mother's left arm, close to the heart. This emphasized the maternal aspect, the dedication and self-giving. At the same time her posture and the features of her face took on a more maternal warmth, and her gaze focused on the child close at hand. The Virgin of Nájera or of Santa María la Blanca at Villasirga provide examples of this change in emphasis. Throughout this period Mary is still shown seated with a fruit or flower, in allusion to the new creation, in her right hand.

In the high Gothic of the late thirteenth century, Mary ceases to be portrayed as seated, and is shown standing, crushing the dragon or serpent that represents evil. Christ is still held in her left arm. This is the figure of the Woman of the Apocalypse: not only the Seat of Wisdom, not only the mother – this is the beautiful Woman who brought the Saviour into the world; she is the New Eve, the Queen and Lady who intercedes for her children, even at the Last Judgement (as in the tympanum of León cathedral's central doorway). These three basic stages in the development of the artistic representation of the figure of Mary are always with us on the *Camino de Santiago* in the different images of her that we meet. She becomes our constant companion, and from Sahagún onwards she becomes a pilgrim. The ancient Franciscan church there is called La Peregrina, and the image of Mary in pilgrim guise is today in the museum of the Benedictine convent. We also find Mary venerated as a pilgrim in Santiago and in Pontevedra. Another name that reflects the same devotion is that of Santa María del Camino, or the Virgen del Camino, as in Pamplona, Carrión de los Condes and León. Mary is venerated by these titles in many Spanish villages.

Mary depicted as a pilgrim really signifies that God has

united himself to humankind, that through the workings of the natural world and a human way of life, he transmits the message of his nearness, of his companionship, of his hope.

Consolation on the Road

God consoles us on the Road;
We only have to be aware
That the Road is our condition.
Life as a whole and all that one needs
Should be a shanty for the wanderer,
Not a house to settle down in.
Imagine that a stretch of road is behind you,
And that another stretch is still ahead of you to do.
If you dawdle, let it be to catch your second wind,
Not a prelude to falling by the wayside.

From St Augustine's Commentary on Psalm 34.4

Pilgrimage is Encounter

The Hospitalité Saint Jacques at Estaing on the Le Puy route through south-western France was established in 1992 to care for pilgrims on their way to Compostela. This Christian community's three founders live out this mission in a spirit of unconditional welcome and personal encounter. The encounter works both ways, as the following extracts from a talk by a member of the community demonstrate:

Pilgrims are a good sample of humankind with their interior riches, their deep aspirations and their sorrows . . . The daily exercise of our faith is to recognize in each pilgrim the presence of Christ himself. In this dual action it is difficult to know who is giving and who is receiving (the word 'hôte' in French means both guest and host). We have to live this as a constant exchange. What we offer to a pilgrim's existential fragility – a roof, some comfort, an encounter in an atmosphere of peace and prayer – is given back to us a hundredfold, both materially and in the unquantifiable ways of the Spirit . . . So this mission of welcome is a privilege, a grace. It has transformed our lives and we hope that it will continue to transform them.

In keeping with the universality of the *Camino* that was affirmed even in the Middle Ages, pilgrims of every background today find a welcome at the Hospitalité Saint Jacques, since the community believes that 'accueils (places of welcome) . . . are in the most authentic jacobean tradition, but also derive their legitimacy from a deep respect for the spiritual liberty of every pilgrim. Opening their doors to all, believers or not, Christians or followers of other religions, they are at the service of all who walk the Way, without discrimination.'

And yet, the Hospitalité Saint Jacques is not simply a place of welcome: it also has 'a mission to accompany the pilgrim, notably through prayer'. This it carries out by daily communal prayer for all the pilgrims who have passed through in the previous two months, reading their names aloud, entrusting them to the loving care of St James, and in this sense accompanying them as they make their way towards Compostela.

Quotations from Marie-Claude Piton's presentation to the Confraternity of Saint James at its Second International Conference, Body and Soul: Hospitality Through the Ages on the Camino de Santiago *(Canterbury, 2001), translated by William Griffiths.*

Route of brotherhood

It is in the relationship with the other
Where a person forges character
And where, as in a mirror,
He or she can see reflected
The movements of the spirit.

Self-awareness
Only grows in dialogue with the other,
Weaving friendship
As participation and communication
Of the most precious gift, which is faith.
The Way of St James
Has to be a 'route of brotherhood',
As a space, time and spiritual setting
In which Catholics may tell about
Their faith and their hope (1 Pet. 3.15),
And foster ecumenical dialogue
With their separated brothers,
With the members of other religions
And also with those
Who do not live the joy of faith
And who, in a spirit of seeking,
Come asking questions and inwardly enquiring
From one end of the route
To the other.

Julián Barrio Barrio, Archbishop of Santiago de Compostela,
'Peregrinar en espiritu y en verdad' (Pilgrims in spirit and in truth),
pastoral letter for the Compostellan Holy Year 1999, Santiago de
Compostela, 1999, p. 24 (translated by Laurie Dennett).

Part 11
The Doorway of Forgiveness

THE ROUTE

From Ponferrada to Lugo

➡ Ponferrada: the city is situated on the banks of the rivers Boeza and Sil. Osmundo, Bishop of Astorga, built an iron bridge (*Pons Ferrata*) over the Sil in the eleventh century, and from this Ponferrada takes its name. The town became an obligatory halt for pilgrims to Santiago but had earlier been an important settlement for the Romans and the Asturians. Theodoric destroyed it in the fifth century, as did troops from Cordoba in the ninth, after which Alfonso III 'el Magno' rebuilt it. Following the repopulation carried out by Fernando II of León, on the site of a Roman encampment, the Order of the Knights Templar began the construction of the castle (1178), which still exists. In 1185 Fernando II gave the growing town to the Templars, under whose care it flourished until the Order was dissolved in 1312 by Pope Clement V. The Templars apparently discovered an image of the Virgin Mary in a holm oak while felling it during the building of the castle, and thus began the veneration of Nuestra Señora de la Encina, the patroness of the Bierzo region. The existing image dates from the first half of the sixteenth century, and the basilica (which gained its status in 1958) was built between 1573 and 1660. The city's other monuments include the Hospital de la Reina, which queen Isabella 'la Catolica' ordered to be built in 1498; the church of San Andrés (seventeenth century); the convent of the Concepcionistas or Sisters of the Immaculate Conception, dating from 1542; the seventeenth-century ayuntamiento or town hall; and the complex formed by the Torre del Reloj (Clock Tower), arch and former gaol, now a museum (sixteenth century). There are other monuments in the area, among them the ninth- and tenth-century Mozarabic church of Santo Tomás de las Ollas and the eleventh-century one of Santa María de Vizbayo, with Mozarabic

The cross with the symbols of 'Alpha' and 'Omega': church of San Pedro de Montes, near Ponferrada.

remains. In the mountains outside the city are Peñalba de Santiago, a tenth-century Mozarabic church, and the ruins of the monastery of San Pedro de Montes, founded in the seventh century by San Fructuoso and restored in 895 by San Genadio, with Visigothic, Romanesque and later remains – San Valerio lived here in the eighth century. The place fell into disrepair following the sequestration of church property in the nineteenth century.

→ Camponaraya: recent archaeological discoveries attest to the long history of this town on the banks of the river Cúa, which traditionally has been closely associated with the pilgrimage. It had a hospital dedicated to St Lazarus and a chapel to St Roch. Rebuilt by the dynamic Archbishop of Compostela, Diego Gelmírez, in 1108, it enjoyed the protection of the see of Compostela until well into the nineteenth century. There is a church dedicated to San Ildefonso of Toledo. That of Santa María de la Plaza, sixteenth century, has a Romanesque chapel and a thirteenth-century stone statue of the Virgin. On the way out of town is the eighteenth-century sanctuary of the Quinta Angustia or 'Fifth Sorrow' (the original building was documented even in the thirteenth century), which has a relief on the door of the sacristy showing the child Jesus playing cards with St Augustine. There is also an archaeological museum.

→ Outside the city lie the ruins of the Roman *Castrum Bergidum*, from which the area known as Las Médulas was administered. There was also a Suevian camp at Pieros, whose church of San Martín was built in 1086 by Osmundo, Bishop of Astorga. A further historic site is that of *Castro Venosa*, which was taken under the protection of Alfonso IX in 1209.

Las Médulas, León: where the Romans once mined gold for the Empire.

→ Las Médulas: this area lies off the *Camino*, but it shaped the history of the region. In his *Historia Naturalis* Pliny the Elder describes how the Romans obtained the gold from this enclave in the mountains of the Bierzo. Vast reservoirs of water and a network of tunnels measuring some 130 kilometres, the digging of which was carried out by both freemen and slaves, were used to wash out the precious metal, and when the ore was exhausted, to destroy the mines, producing the singular *Ruina Montium* we see today. In this context the *Ruta de la Plata* (Silver Route) seems to have arisen, to coincide later with the *Camino Mozarabe* to Santiago.

→ Villafranca del Bierzo: Alfonso VI founded this Frankish settlement on the banks of the river Burbia, with the aid of Cluny. The existing collegiate church of Santa María de

Cruñego has a sixteenth-century altarpiece. It is documented as having had a chapter of canons between 1529 and 1862 and is situated on top of the earlier church built by the Cluniac monks and dedicated to Santa María de Cluny. The town became the property of the Osorio family, the head of which was ennobled in 1486 with the title of Marques of Villafranca. Between 1822 and 1853 the town of Villafranca was the capital of the Bierzo. In the outskirts and near the cemetery the *Camino* passes the twelfth-century Romanesque church of Santiago with its Puerta del Perdón or 'doorway of Forgiveness', arising from a privilege conceded by Pope Calixtus III (1455–58) whereby pilgrims who through ill-health were unable to reach Compostela could obtain the jubilee indulgence here, as if they had. There is an interesting depiction of the Three Wise Men on this doorway. Close by, on the site of the former hospital dedicated to San Lázaro, stands a modern pilgrim hostel or *albergue*. The church of San Francisco recalls the saint's stay here on his pilgrimage to Compostela: it has a Romanesque doorway, fourteenth-century apse and sixteenth-century Mudejar ceiling. Other historic buildings are: the castle and palace of the Marquis of Villafranca, begun in 1514; the Franciscan convent, known as La Anunciada and dating from 1606, with a seventeenth-century altarpiece and tomb of the Italian saint Lawrence of Brindisi; the former Jesuit college of San Nicolás in the baroque style of the seventeenth century – the statue of Christ known as el Cristo de la Esperanza, patron of Villafranca, is venerated in the church. Of the five ancient hospitals, that of Santiago remains, converted into a school called La Divina Pastora or 'Divine Shepherdess'. The *Camino* crosses the ancient *Calle del Agua*, where the palaces of the Torquemada and Alvarez de Toledo families stand, together with the chapel of the Omañas. Crossing the damaged medieval bridge over the river Burbia, the route passes the convent of the order founded by Santa Beatríz de Silva. Famous sons of Villafranca include Fray Martín Sarmiento and the writer Enrique Gil y Carrasco.

➔ Corullón: this has two Romanesque churches, San Miguel and San Esteban, and the remains of a fifteenth-century castle.

The nearby village of San Fiz de Visonia has a Romanesque church founded by San Fructuoso in the sixth century that later belonged to the Order of St John.

➡ Valley of the Valcarce: the route carries on against the direction in which the river Valcarce is flowing. Its name derives from the Latin *valle carcer, carceris*, 'prison valley' or 'valley without an exit'. Pereje, a few kilometres on, belonged to the monks of O Cebreiro between 1118 and the confisca-

Pilgrim graffiti on a motorway pillar near Vega de Valcarce, on the border of León and Galicia.

tion of church property in the nineteenth century, having been given to them by Queen Urraca for the support of pilgrims. Trabadelo belonged to the see of Compostela through a similar donation by Alfonso III in 895. The way passes through the territories once overseen by the castle of Auctares, the *Uttuaris* of Antoninus, which was destroyed by Alfonso VI for having exacted tolls from pilgrims. Other points on the route are Portela, Ambasmestas ('place where two currents mingle') and Vega de Valcarce, the town at the top of the valley. Two castles once stood nearby: Sarracín, founded by Saraceno, Count of Astorga, which has ruins dating from the fifteenth century, and Veiga, of which nothing at all remains. Ruitelan was the penitential refuge of San Froilan (833–905), Bishop of León and Lugo. Herrerías was the site of Hospital Inglés, the hospital for English pilgrims (but whether it was built for them or by them is not known) mentioned in a bull issued by Pope Alexander III in 1178. La Faba was frequently mentioned in early pilgrim guides. It and Laguna de Castilla are the last villages in the diocese of Astorga and the province of León.

→ O Cebreiro: this is the gateway to Galicia, from an altitude of 1,293 metres, the point at which waters flow into the Bierzo to the south and into Galicia to the north. Since ancient times it has been a halt for pilgrims and travellers. Early in the seventeenth century the Benedictine historian Dom Antonio Yepes affirmed from documents known to him that there was an inn for pilgrims here as early as 825. In 1072 Alfonso VI entrusted the care of pilgrims to the monks of the reformed Benedictine community founded by the French saint Geraud d'Aurillac. The church and monastery they built were taken over in 1496 by the Benedictine congregation based in Valladolid, and remained part of it until the nineteenth century. The pre-Romanesque church dates from the ninth and tenth centuries and is dedicated to Santa María la Real. Worthy of note are the twelfth-century chalice and paten associated with the eucharistic miracle of Cebreiro, which took place early in the fourteenth century. Its importance is such that the chalice and paten appear in the shields of Galicia and in those of the province and the city of Lugo. According to tradition, the simple faith of a peasant from the nearby village of Barxamaior, contrasting with the little faith of the monk celebrating Mass, set the scene for the transformation of the eucharistic elements of bread and wine into the Body and Blood of Christ. The event passed into legend and the chalice became known as 'the Holy Grail of Galicia' – not to be confused with the Holy Grail of the Last Supper. The Catholic Monarchs, Ferdinand and Isabella, gave the church the reliquary still on view today, to safeguard the relics of the miracle. In the apse of the left aisle of the church is the tomb of Don Elias Valiña Sampedro, the former parish priest of O Cebreiro and the great defender of the

Camino. The whole village is of ethnographical interest, with its museum and its *pallozas* or traditional Celtic dwellings.

➡️ Liñares: the route passes through this village, 'a place from which linen was obtained', whose existence was documented as early as 714. Below the road lies Lagua de Tablas, the home of many knights of the Order of Santiago. Ahead lie Alto de San Roque, where there was once a chapel; Hospital da Condesa, founded by Egilo, wife of Count Gatón, who repopulated this area and the Bierzo; Padornelo, whose church of San Juan was founded by knights of the Order of Malta and later belonged to the see of Compostela; and Alto de Poio, some 1,335 metres above sea level. The way carries on through Fonfria then forks off to the right, traversing Biduedo (where there is a tiny chapel dedicated to San Pedro), and rejoins the road to pass through Filloval, As Pasantes and Ramil.

➡️ Triacastela: the town with its parish church of Santiago and medieval remains once possessed three castles. It was repopulated by Count Gatón, who founded a monastery in honour of saints Peter and Paul, which in 922 was given to the church of Santiago by Ordoño II as an offering for the soul of his wife. Alfonso IX planned that Triacastela should become a large town, but it never did. In 1112 Diego Gelmírez, Archbishop of Compostela, accompanied queen Urraca this far on her way to engage Alfonso I 'el Batallador' in battle. Apparently in the remains of one of the town's pilgrim hospitals, also used for a time as a gaol, there can be seen graffiti made by pilgrims and prisoners. There is a tradition that it was from the quarries near Triacastela that pilgrims carried stones to the ovens at Castañeda to make the lime used in the construction of the cathedral of Santiago de Compostela.

➡️ Leaving Triacastela, the route bifurcates: one branch, the one mentioned in the *Codex Calixtinus*, goes by way of San Gil, Alto de Riocabo, Montán, Fontearcuda, Furela, Pintín, Calvor (whose church of San Esteban has Visigothic remains), Aguiada, San Mamede do Camiño, San Pedro do Camiño, Carballal y Vigo de Sarria to reach Sarria. The other follows the course of the river Oribio towards the monastery dedicated to San Julián and Santa Basilisa (a married couple from Antioch, martyred) at Samos, founded by San Martín Dumiense in the sixth century. A Visigothic slab in the cloister attests to its age. At Samos there is also a ninth- and tenth-century Mozarabic chapel known by the name of San Salvador del Ciprés. The existing monastery buildings date mainly from the sixteenth and seventeenth centuries, with some earlier remains; its cloisters, one with the so-called Nereid fountain, the other featuring a statue of the Benedictine scholar and teacher Jerónimo Feijoo (1676–1774), who taught here, are justly famous.

→ Sarria: this is a town predating the Roman period, known to have been repopulated in 750 by Odoario, Bishop of Lugo. Alfonso IX, who died here in 1230, developed it considerably. Illustrious figures born here include the mystical writer Fray Luis de Granada and the sculptor Gregorio Fernández. Notable among its monuments are the church of Santa Marina (a Galician martyr), the church of San Salvador, the hospital of San Antonio (today the courthouse), the chapel of San Lázaro, the fortress (frequently fought over in medieval times) and the monastery of the Magdalena (today occupied

Wayside cross in Sarria. These sculptural crosses, or cruceiros, *are a common sight in Galicia.*

by the Mercedarian Fathers but originally founded by Italian Augustinians).

→ The route leaves the town by way of the Aspera bridge over the river Celeiro and continues on through San Miguel, Barbadelo (where there is a Romanesque church dedicated to Santiago), Rente, Mercado da Serra, Marzán, Pena Leiman, Peruscallo, Cortiñas, Lavandeira, Casal, Brea, Morgade, Ferreiros, Cruceiro, Mirallos, Pena, Couto, Rozas, Moimentos,

Cotarela, Mercadoiro, Moutrás, Parrocha, Vilachá; this last village is close to the monastery of Loio, home of the monk Quintilla in the ninth century and the property of the Order of St James in 1170.

→ Portomarín: situated on the banks of the river Miño, the town was already documented in 993 as *Villa Portumarini* and referred to as *Pons Minée* by Aymeric Picaud. Its bridge was

destroyed by queen Urraca during her contests with her husband Alfonso I 'el Batallador', and rebuilt by one Pedro Peregrino so that pilgrims could once again cross the river. The town belonged to the Order of the Knights of St John. Another bridge was built in 1929, but the existing one dates from 1962, when the valley was flooded by the creation of the Belesar reservoir. The entire town was moved to higher ground on the west bank, the old one being engulfed by the waters. This is an area

An 'hórreo', or grain store, on the Camino near Portomarín.

closely associated with the pilgrimage, where pilgrims are received with traditional hospitality. Part of the old bridge is preserved near the new one, with the chapel of the Virgen de las Nieves. The stones of the facade of the church of San Pedro (1182) and that of the Romanesque fortress-church of San Nicolás were numbered to aid reconstruction when the town was moved, and the numbers can be clearly seen both here and on the casa del Conde and the palace of Berbetoros.

Our itinerary takes us to Lugo, although that city does not figure in the *Codex Calixtinus*.

STOP AND THINK ABOUT IT

'Lift up your heads, O ye gates; and be ye lift up, ye everlasting doors; and the King of glory shall come in.' With those words from Psalm 24, verse 7, used in the liturgy in the time leading up to Christmas, we express the hope of finding doors open within ourselves and in others. We know, furthermore, how hard it is to open inner and outer doors – and in the same way the experience of standing before closed doors and portals is one we have all had.

On the Way of St James we often come upon doors and gateways small and large, Romanesque and Gothic, simple and ornate, adorned with symbols and damaged by the passage of time, closed and wide open. Here in the church of Santiago of Villafranca del Bierzo we find the second of the three Puertas del Perdón or doorways of forgiveness (the first being that of San Isidoro in León) on the *Camino de Santiago*. The third is the Puerta Santa or Holy Door that ushers pilgrims into the cathedral of Santiago, and is only opened during Compostellan Holy Years. These doorways of forgiveness invite us to reflect on the door as symbol.

The Doorway – a Sign that Speaks

We have all had personal experiences that have had to do with doors. If I allow myself time, the words 'entrance' or 'door' easily recall memories of many doorways or where one or another, at a specific moment or perhaps in my present life, may be playing an important role: a closed door or an open one, lightweight or heavy, low or high, the main way in or the back entrance, the door to the cellar or to the stable, a glass door or the door of a church. What features does it have? Where does it lead? What feelings and experiences do I associate with it?

Experience tells us that a door, an entrance, a portal, a portico are articulate signs that have hidden meanings.

A door may open and close, invite and exclude, reject

and encourage, be ajar or shut tight, offer free passage or be blocked. It separates that which is inside from that which is outside. Space becomes limited and even private once a threshold is passed. My state of being on the *Camino* changes on reaching a door, and goes from breadth to inwardness, to being indoors, at home; to being in a smaller, more enclosed place.

Door, entrance, portal and portico awaken curiosity, sometimes fear, at what may be revealed, and yet they establish an order. Exterior confusion and menace are kept outside. Some doorways invite us to enter, to relax, to feel ourselves secure, to find our own centre, our interior peace.

Each of us can be a doorway, open or closed, inviting or rejecting, welcoming or prickly, a bearer of peace or hostility. One can become a liberating entryway or a threshold that is impassable.

Who has been a door for me?

For whom have I been able to be a door?

Door, entrance, portal and portico are signs that speak, that we encounter every day: living symbols of human community. They are also symbols of reconciliation.

The Doorway of Forgiveness

We stand before a Doorway of Forgiveness. These had an outstanding place in the history of the Way of St James. Pilgrims, sometimes sick to the point of death and too weak to continue, received here the consolation of being able to be freed from their sins and temporal punishments as if they had reached Santiago, their journey's end. For them, to pass through this doorway meant the forgiveness of their sins, reconciliation with themselves and with Christ, the judge of the world.

Why is that privilege particularly associated with this place?

Various sources suggest that in this area earlier cultures worshipped local pagan gods. Even today there is talk of supernatural forces. Not far from here was the *Castrum Bergidum*, which administered the mines of Las Médulas. Slaves who succeeded in escaping and reaching it would be granted their freedom since the Romans accepted it as a place of worship and sanctuary and respected the local deities. Comparing it with similar contexts it may well be that Christianity adopted this usage, conceding to sick pilgrims the means of freeing themselves from their sins as if they had reached Santiago. These pilgrims experienced the reality of Jesus' words when he said: 'I am the door: by me if any man enter in, he shall be saved' (John 10.9).

Jesus' invitation is equally valid for today's pilgrims. They are invited to leave behind their faults and hindrances in order to enter by the door and at the same time to be persons who open the door for others.

BETWEEN PAST AND PRESENT

Romanesque Doorways – a Visual System and its Structure

The door of a church marks the limit between sacred and profane space, between the interior and the exterior, between one side and the other. The space to which the door gives access becomes a Christian church of God when the bishop blesses the building. On this occasion the bishop, with crozier and mitre, approaches the new church in solemn procession with members of the Christian community. On arrival, before its closed doors, he asks a deacon or one of the concelebrating priests to open them. Then the psalm is sung, 'Lift up your heads, O ye gates; and be ye lift up, ye everlasting doors; and the King of glory shall come in' (Ps. 24.9). And all enter, led by the bishop.

In past times, according to ritual, the bishop also anointed the doorjambs with chrism while he uttered the words: 'Portal, be consecrated and at the service of God. Be an entrance for peace through Him who called Himself the Gateway.' In the Romanesque era a reliquary was placed under the threshold to protect the sacred space from profanation. The threshold was central. It had a double mission: rejection, admonition and defence on the one hand; invitation, guidance and promise on the other.

We find this duality in Romanesque doorways in a variety of expressions. Without losing ourselves in the details we can discern the following fundamental construction: the idea of rejection, admonition and defence is situated on the left part of the portal. Temptation, carnality, the devil and sin are frequently represented here. The right part in contrast is reserved for the saints, the chosen, the redeemed and their symbols. They invite, indicate the way and promise eternal salvation.

The same principle serves for the arrangement of subjects from bottom to top. Facing the human vices, the demons and the monsters, are those who announce the faith, the martyrs, and those who have triumphed over earthly temptations. On the lintel we find, depending on the local references, different biblical scenes such as Adam and Eve being expelled from Eden, the Last Supper, the Apostles gathered at Pentecost or at the Ascension. The central column of the doorway, which divides its lower part, concentrates on the symbols that refer to the totality of creation. We find it very clearly stated in the Pórtico de la Gloria of the cathedral of Santiago: from the animals in the base humankind emerges, and from among them springs the root and Tree of Jesse and upon it, seated, St James welcomes pilgrims. He has been fashioned in a similar manner to Christ (above him in the tympanum), and wears an expression that says, 'You have arrived at last. Enter into the glory of your Lord. I am only his servant and have accompanied you on the *Camino*.'

The central point and the crown of the Romanesque doorway – and this is clearly visible in the example of Santiago – is the tympanum: the semi-circle situated above the lintel. With different variations the central theme is always presented: Christ is the Lord and the judge over all life and death; his power and glory have no limits. The semi-circle and the richly carved rib-vaults forming arches symbolize heaven, the earthly image of which one enters on stepping through the doorway into the church. The tympanum is supported on the jambs and adjoining stonework with their columns, figures and capitals, the ornamentation of which corresponds by and large to the principle already mentioned regarding left and right, upper and lower.

This basic structure in the Romanesque is very varied, and on each occasion its figures (animals, monsters, angels, prophets, Apostles) and symbols (nature, death, fabulous beings, demons) are arranged and adapted in a new unity. The person who regards them closely is left full of admiration for the whole and impressed by details that are perpetually fresh; that speak to him all the way along the *Camino de Santiago* of human faith and hope.

Christ and the 'Four Living Creatures'

In the doorways of the churches of the *Camino de Santiago* we find repeatedly the four living creatures that surround the throne of the Lord of the universe. They remind us of St John's description of the Apocalypse (John 4.7–9). These four living creatures (in Greek, *tetramorphos*) are usually, as in the writings of St Jerome, taken as the symbols of the four evangelists: the man (St Matthew), the lion (St Mark) the ox (St Luke) and the eagle (St John). This interpretation has entered deeply into history and art.

The origin of the four living creatures lies in a vision in chapter 1 of the prophet Ezekiel paraphrased here: 'From out of a whirlwind came a shape like four living creatures . . . they had human form. Each one had four faces and four wings. Regarding their faces, one was the face of a man, and each of the four had the face of a lion to the right, the face of an ox to the left, and the four also had the face of an eagle.' These four creatures are those normally represented in the tympana of doorways in relation to the risen Christ, the Lord of time and the eternal judge. As Lord of the universe, he looks in all directions and his sovereignty extends to the 'four corners of the earth'.

Christ and the 'Four Living Beings' on the south door of the church of Santa María la Real, Sangüesa.

This idea is presented even more clearly in a Latin gospel dating from the fourteenth century that in essence repeats the interpretations of the four creatures offered by Iraneaus of Lyons (second century) and Gregory the Great (sixth century): 'These four creatures represent Christ, the Lord. He is man in his birth, ox in the sacrifice of his death, lion in the resurrection, eagle in his ascension.' Here, nature, the cosmos and the work of salvation are succinctly summarized, and the Romanesque conception of the world and of Christ is clearly stated.

Part 12
The Wayside Crosses

THE ROUTE

From Lugo to Santiago

➡ Leaving Portomarín, the *Camino* passes through Toxibo, Gonzar, Castromaior and Hospital (the name recalls the Hospital of the Cross that existed here) to Ventas de Narón, where it intersects the paved highway that traces the route of the ancient Roman thoroughfare that ran from Lugo to Braga.

➡ Lugo: although it is not the classic Way of St James according to the *Codex Calixtinus*, many pilgrims followed the road from Astorga to Lugo, while many also travelled by way of Asturias and passed through Lugo on what today is called the Camino Primitivo. Lugo, a provincial capital with a 2,000-year history, situated at the site of hot springs and the banks of the river Miño, is said to take its name from Lu, the god of fire. Another view is that the name derives from *Lucus Augusti*, the Roman name for the settlement established on the site of a former encampment from which the northern region of Galicia had been administered, linked by important roads to Astorga and Braga. The city's defensive walls were built in the third century but did not prevent the slaughter carried out by the Suevians in 462 or the destruction wrought by the Moorish commander Muza in 714. In 569 Lugo hosted an important church council. Alfonso I, who liberated Lugo, ceded rank to its Bishop, Odoario. Later, San Froilán (833–905) was Bishop and patron of the city. For centuries it remained within its Roman wall, some 2,100 metres long and possessed of 72 low watchtowers. Notable is the Puerta de Santiago, dating from 1759. The cathedral, with a neoclassical facade, was begun in a transitional Romanesque-Gothic style in 1229 by Bishop Pedro Peregrino; the construction went on until the fourteenth century. The Blessed Sacrament is permanently exposed on the high altar, a privilege dating from time immemorial. Among the chapels, that of Nuestra Señora de los Ojos Grandes, a Gothic image in a baroque setting dating from 1720, is particularly worthy of note. In the transepts are pieces of a sixteenth-century altarpiece by Cornelius de Holanda. The splendid choirstalls are by the eighteenth-century Galician artist Fernando de Moure. Outside, over the north door is a Christ in Majesty with a pendant sculpture depicting the Last Supper (thirteenth century). Other important city monuments include: the Plaza de Santa María and the bishop's palace; the Franciscan monastery; the provincial museum (situated in another former monastery); the Augustinian convent in the Plaza de Santo Domingo; the Plaza Mayor and the eighteenth-century ayuntamiento or town hall at its eastern end.

➡️ Returning to the point on the *Camino Francés* where we left off in the previous chapter, the route from Ventas de Naron goes on to Ligonde, which was an important pilgrim halt, with a church of Santiago and a hospital. Eirexe (with Romanesque remains) is next, a parish that belonged to San Marcos of León; then Portos.

➡️ Vilar de Doñas: the village stands a little way off the route with its church of El Salvador, which in 1184 came into the possession of the Order of Santiago and became the place where knights who died in Galicia were buried. A convent that existed here two centuries earlier explains the 'Doñas' or 'ladies' of the name. The church is Romanesque, the baldachin or canopy fifteenth century; there is a small stone frontal over the altar and fifteenth-century wall paintings depicting various religious themes and the founding 'ladies', Bela and Elvira, and possibly also King Juan II and his queen, María de Aragón. There are various tombstones that mark the burial places of knights of Santiago. Once back on the main road, pilgrims pass through Lestedo.

Palas de Rei: the *Palatium Regis* of the *Codex Calixtinus*; its name probably refers to the king's visits to the tombs of the knights of Santiago since he was the Grand Master of their order and had to stay nearby. The town has a church dedicated to San Tirso, with a Romanesque doorway. It is mentioned in the ninth-century 'Caelicolae' of Alfonso III; some scholars consider that it may have been an episcopal see in the fifth century and that the Gothic King Witiza must have based his court here.

The way passes through San Xulián do Camiño with its Romanesque church; legend has it that this saint accidentally killed his parents and assuaged his sin by becoming a *hospitalero* along with his wife Adela, until an angel brought news of divine forgiveness. Near Porto Bois is the site of the battle waged by the Trastámara against the duke of Lemos, who supported Pedro I 'el Cruel'. In Coto the route leaves the province of Lugo and enters that of La Coruña, continuing on through Cornixa to Leboreiro – the *Campus Levurarius* (Hares' Field) of the *Codex Calixtinus*, with its Romanesque-Gothic church of Santa María – and Disicabo to Furelos, with its bridge, church of San Juan, ancient hospital and a rectory that was once the *encomienda* or manor house.

A Roman bridge, still in use after two millennia at Ferreira, Galicia.

➡ Melide/Mellid: pilgrims coming from Oviedo via Sobrado de los Monjes joined the *Camino Francés* here. The town is of Celtic origin; it has two Romanesque churches: San Pedro, with a splendid doorway, and Santa María, with sixteenth-century wall paintings. There was once a monastery and hospital, built in the fourteenth century on the site of an earlier foundation, of which the existing church of San Pedro and the ayuntamiento formed a part. By way of Boente the route continues.

➡ Castañeda: site of the ovens where lime was manufactured for the construction of the cathedral of Santiago. It was the custom for pilgrims to pick up stones in Triacastela to carry this far, as a contribution to this process, as Aymeric Picaud relates.

➡ Ribadiso: here there was once a fifteenth-century hospital dedicated to San Antón.

➡ Arzua: this has a convent dedicated to Santa María Magdalena, a fourteenth-century Augustinian foundation that had a pilgrim hospital. Today there is a modern church of Santiago, and in the outskirts a chapel of San Lázaro that recalls a former hospital.

➡ The *Camino* carries on through small settlements, among them As Barrosas, Calzada, Calle, Brea, Santa Irene, Arca do Pino and Amenal, to emerge near the airport, which it skirts since the ancient track has been obliterated by the present landing strip.

➡ Lavacolla: in medieval times this was known as *Lavamentula*, since here the pilgrims washed themselves all over and hurried on, eager to gain the honour of being the first to see the spires of the cathedral in the distance (tra-

A pump has replaced the stream that was the traditional washing place at Lavacolla, the last stop before Santiago.

dition has it that the first pilgrim in any group to see them gained the right to change their surname to King or its French, German or Italian equivalent).

➡ Monte del Gozo: near the chapel of San Marcos is the hill from which the joyful sight of the cathedral and city of the Apostle can be seen.

➡ The way passes through the parish of San Lázaro, where there was a leper hospital founded in the twelfth century; then into the neighbourhood known as the Barrio de Concheiros ('scallop-shell wearers') and down the Rua de San Pedro de Foras (from *fuera*, 'outside the walls', since within them there already existed San Pedro de Antealtares, later San Paio). It reaches Puerta del Camino (or Porta do Camiño in the language of Galicia), also known as the Porta Francigena, and traces its way through the Rúa dos Casas Reales, Rúa das Animas, Plaza de Cervantes with its fountain, and Azabachería; here was situated the Plaza del Paraíso of the *Codex Calixtinus*, today bearing the name of the Inmaculada Concepción. Pilgrims are now only steps away from the cathedral.

Stop and Think About It

On the road, travellers and pilgrims need guidance and waymarks. There are maps, signs indicating villages and information about roads and distances, but above all there are waymarks specific to the *Camino de Santiago*: the yellow arrows, the blue signs put up by the Council of Europe with their various symbols (pilgrim, scallop-shell, star), the stone markers, the plaques erected to commemorate some ruined chapel or lonely church, and the wayside crosses, or *cruceiros*. All of them are means of orientation. Let's pause a moment to reflect on the well-known feature of the route, the wayside crosses.

A Universal Symbol

The cross is a universal symbol predating Christianity. We know of various forms of the cross, but the oldest is the one with all four arms of equal length, surrounded by a circle. In this form the cross is an ancient representation of the cardinal directions, of the light and the sun, of the four seasons of the year and, later, of Christ as light, of his universal dominion, of the four evangelists and so on.

At the point of intersection the cross is composed of a vertical line and a horizontal one: the first connects what comes from above with what comes from below, the other unites left and right. It is therefore a symbol of encounter and connection, of centring and mediation, but it also suggests separation, and with this, the need for decision. The cross unites points that are opposites and that strain to break apart, and thus becomes a symbol for humanity itself, in which are brought together the high and the low, the right and the left, the head and the feet, the captive and the free, the body and the spirit, birth and death, the conscious and the unconscious.

A Christian Symbol

As a Christian symbol – think of the Latin cross with its elongated vertical and shortened horizontal lines – the cross became ever more important. Until the sixth century it bore no crucified figure. Along the *Camino de Santiago* we find the Visigothic cross, using the ancient symbolism that recalls the manner in which it was used by the Romans as an instrument of punishment, of execution and death. The Visigoths added the Christian interpretation. The cross of execution and death became, then, the symbol of redemption and victory. The cross met death head on and was transformed into the sign of the road to follow: 'Whosoever will come after me, let him deny himself, and take up his cross, and follow me' (Mark 8.34).

A Symbol of Life

The cross at the same time symbolizes each and every individual. In the first place we see this with reference to the body, which is composed of a vertical axis (the spinal column) uniting two crosses (the legs and arms), surmounted by the head. Such a basic appreciation may help us to understand our physical functioning and how important are harmony, balance and poise in the way we carry ourselves

But the crosses we encounter on the *Camino* can also symbolize:

- **Meeting and encounter:** the destiny and good fortune of pilgrims, the highs and lows of the journey, the act of requesting and the gratitude of receiving. The sign of the cross and of St James, the first martyr among the Apostles, has united pilgrims from all over the world. Each cross on the Way invites recollection, prayer, encounter with others, so that what is separate may be united in the enacting of pilgrimage.

- **Crossroads:** every day we encounter contradictions and the need for decisions. The ways coming from different directions meet, join together for a brief space of time and often separate again, as pilgrims' lives do on the *Camino*. We all recognize situations when hopes and wishes, plans and circumstances intersect and become weighty and painful. Such 'crosses' have many names: loneliness, illness, affliction, disappointment, separation, unemployment, lack of meaning, distrust. But these crosses in life also bear the stamp of the cross of Christ. We only have to recall the original meaning of this: the cross doesn't represent Golgotha, but the return of the risen Christ who even in his public life dedicated himself especially to those who had 'crosses' to carry. Christ's cross is the true sign of solidarity and hope.

- **Decision:** when paths cross we are forced to decide which one to follow. When we find ourselves at a crossroads in life we experience interior tensions because very often, instead of going to the heart of the matter, we grope our way towards reaching a decision. The cross is the symbol of hope that overcomes perplexity and lack of advice and invites us to centre ourselves, to gather our strength, open ourselves and carry on, placing our trust in Christ crucified and resurrected.

Crossroads

He came where four roads meet
He chose a narrow one;
Spring thorns the way beset
But at the end there shone
The bright reward that pilgrims get

And Heaven's unsetting sun.

John Davidson

BETWEEN PAST AND PRESENT

St James in Art

By way of the pilgrimage route, the image of St James (in Hebrew, *Ya' aqov'el*, 'God protects') became omnipresent in the religious and cultural lives of medieval people, not only of those on the *Camino* but throughout Europe. Biblical tradition (and in particular, legends), together with medieval religious sentiment and concept of pilgrimage, largely determined the way he was represented. These images served to make the figure of St James and his message – his life, works and death and their meaning for the 'road' of life of each individual or community – more accessible to a populace that was mainly illiterate, making him visible, for example, in the facades of churches, in tympana and altarpieces, where he appeared as a single figure or as one of a group. From the twelfth century until the end of the Middle Ages we find various kinds of jacobean references along the Way of St James, with some specific features that are at the same time typical.

- **St James the Apostle:** we find him in very ancient representations without any special attributes, with a tunic or a toga, barefoot and holding a book or rolled document, as in Sangüesa, or in the *Codex Calixtinus*. He is not depicted any differently from the other Apostles. He was identified by the addition of his name or by his position in the iconographic scheme of the particular facade or church. We see him depicted this way on the right-hand side of the Pórtico de la Gloria of the cathedral of Santiago, conversing with his brother John and holding a staff in the form of the *tau*, or letter T, indicating that he had completed his journey. His clothing is similar to that of the seated figure of him in the central column, below that of Christ, holding a page that reads *Misit me Dominus* – 'God sent me'. St James is found in an equally notable position in the doorway of the cathedral in the Plaza de Platerías, where he stands to the right of Christ with a book in his hand, between two cypress trees, the biblical symbol of unending fidelity: 'I am like a green fir tree. From me is thy fruit found' (Hos. 14.8). The historian Robert Plötz in his *Imago Beati Jakobi* has delineated the political and ecclesiastical interests of Archbishop Diego Gelmírez in the cathedral's relationship with Toledo and Rome that lie behind this iconographical preference for St James. The figure of St James in the portico of the monastery church of San Salvador de Leyre emphasizes even further his stature as an apostle and

St James in the portico of the monastery church of San Salvador de Leyre.

147

herald of Christ's message. With three fingers of his right hand he witnesses to the trinitarian God (one God but three Persons) and indicates the Good News, while the other two fingers stand for the divine and human nature of Christ, he to whom St James refers. A similar interpretation can be applied to the three fingers of the left hand, which, indicating the Trinity, hold the book and guarantee the truth that St James has received and which he is passing on. The meanings attributed to the fingers and their positions are those most widely held. None the less, it is equally important to emphasize how new forms and characteristics of the representation of St James in art were constantly evolving from the twelfth century onwards, through the medium of the pilgrimage. From being one Apostle among the rest, St James gradually emerged as the Apostle St James of Compostela.

- **St James the martyr**, who bears witness: we find various depictions of the saint in this guise. One of them, not very common on the *Camino*, represents him with the sword that was the instrument of his martyrdom and death. We find him thus in the south door of the cathedral of Chartres and in the Paradise Door of the cathedral of Orense, although the date of the last mentioned figure is uncertain, as Robert Plötz points out in the work noted above. In Germany, St James with a sword is found at Telgte, Ennigerloh and on the reliquary of the Three Kings in Cologne. It seems this representation has nothing to do with the figure of St James at Las Huelgas Reales in Burgos (which had a moveable arm and a hand that held a sword) used to invest the king as the Grand Master of the Order of St James. A different way of portraying St James, though it may be partly related to depictions such as that of Leyre, described above, shows him surrounded by animals and in particular by lions (a meaningful motif in Romanesque art, used to indicate vigilance, courage or good versus evil – qualities shown by St James as the first Apostle to die a martyr). The curled tail of the king of beasts indicates his submissiveness and affirmation of the message of St James: the martyr's witness is true. His violent death does not destroy the message; on the contrary, his martyrdom bears witness to it. When put to the test, he is victorious. We see lions at the feet of St James in the central column of the Pórtico de la Gloria and in the doorway in the Plaza de las Platerías.

- **St James the pilgrim:** we find him seated, standing or in the act of walking in many depictions, as the constant companion of pilgrims on the *Camino*. We recognize him by his broad hat and cloak, staff, pilgrim satchel and water-gourd, and by one or several scallop-shells on his hat, bag or clothing. He does not always display all the attributes. The identifying signs of the pilgrim are sometimes mixed with those of the Apostle. Examples of this occur in the figure of St James in Puente la Reina, who also holds a Bible in his hand; in the altarpiece of the church at Miraflores, near Burgos, St James the pilgrim is reading. In the well-known relief in the eleventh-century cloister at Santo Domingo de Silos discussed earlier, Jesus is depicted as a jacobean pilgrim accompanying the disciples on the road to Emmaus. In the central pillar of the Pórtico de la Gloria of Santiago cathedral, St James, holding a scroll and *tau* staff, receives pilgrims in the name of the Lord and bids them enter. Experience teaches us that for steadiness while walking, a pilgrim needs a long staff, whereas the elderly St James represented here, who has reached his destination, needs the shorter version for balance only. The Church Fathers interpreted the *tau* as a sign of redemption, so that we should rather speak of the pilgrim's staff as signifying a *potential* abundance, rather than a plenitude achieved. Santiago with his *tau* has completed his pilgrimage through this life and has entered into the Kingdom of God. In other depictions St James indicates the scallop-shell as a symbol of the pilgrimage, as in the Puerta del Sarmental in Burgos; or he is shown protecting pilgrims, as in the museum at Roncesvalles and the doors of the Hospital del Rey in Burgos; or mounted, as in the Museo de los Caminos in Astorga and elsewhere. All these show how, along the Way, the figure of St James and the depiction of the pilgrim became steadily more alike until they were virtually identical. Stated slightly differently, the practical equipment of the pilgrim (hat, scrip and staff) that before the development of the Way of St James were typical of travellers in general, became clear emblems for identifying St James the pilgrim in artistic contexts, both in Spain and along the routes leading to it from other parts of Europe.

- **St James, the defender of the faith and so-called *Matamoros*:** It is uncertain, though there are several theories, how much influence the figure of the *miles Christi* or 'soldier of Christ', with his aim of defending the faith, may have had in the evocation of St James in the guise of *Matamoros* or 'Moor slayer'. There is quite a distance between the fisherman of Galilee and the Apostle, and more still between the Apostle and the warrior and defender of the faith. We know of other holy warriors such as St Michael and St George; and other defenders of the faith in Spain, such as San Millán de la Cogolla and San Isidoro, whose images occur along the *Camino*. The image of St James as a warrior is linked to the battle of Clavijo (in 844), which came about because the Christian inhabitants of what is today Navarra and La Rioja refused to pay the tribute of the 100 maidens to their Muslim overlords. (Such payments were a form of vassalage exacted from many towns and areas by the conquerors.) It seems that 'Santiago' was the rallying-cry of the armies assembled for the fight, since the same is said of the battle of Simancas in 922. Artistic references to this include the four bulls whose heads appear as stone capitals in the doorway of Santa María del Camino in Carrión de los Condes, the fiesta of the *Cantadeiras* in León, and the standard from Clavijo that is safeguarded in Astorga. As with many other nationalistic images, it is hard to determine how much is history and how much is legend, but its nebulous origins are no bar to widespread devotion. The depiction of St James mounted on his white charger, routing the enemy, is very well known. In some Spanish towns and regions he is referred to simply as *El Patron* – since he is the patron saint of Spain. One such representation, dating from the twelfth century, can be seen just by the door leading to the cloister, in the right-hand transept of the cathedral of Santiago de Compostela.

This way of portraying St James as 'Moor slayer' or mounted warrior is often felt by foreigners to be exclusively the product of the Iberian peninsula. What is certain is that Christian forces, in their struggle with Muslim opponents (for example, in the Crusades to the Holy Land), were in the habit of sending representations to the Apostle at Compostela before or after a battle, to ask favours or give thanks. In 1147 the English fleet, on its way to the Second Crusade and after passing Galicia, helped the first King of Portugal, Alfonso Enriquez, in the conquest of Lisbon, and when bottled up by a storm in the Tagus estuary and menaced by Muslim forces, sent envoys to entreat the help of St James at Compostela. St Louis of France sent soldiers to offer thanksgiving. In Innsbruck cathedral, in the Austrian Tyrol, and in Bamberg in Germany we also find images of the warrior St James. In the catalogue of an exhibition on St James in Franconia, held in the cathedral of Würzburg in 1993, we are told that the German nobility entrusted their struggle for the Holy Land to St James. There are similar examples and testimonials from parts of Spain during the Reconquista that make it patently clear that St James was seen and appealed to as the protector of the Christian kingdoms during that period. In our own day, social change and political correctness have made these warrior images unappealing, but this should not lead us to deny their origin and historical significance.

Matamoros

The rearing white steed
must forever be held suspended
in his resplendent pose.
The raised sword
must never descend again
to inflict bloody miracles
on infidels.

Santiago
apóstol

mártir
peregrino
   ¡sé paladín de la paz ahora!

                    Karin Temple

St James in all His Guises

St James, son of Zebedee, fisherman on the lake of Galilee
and disciple of Jesus of Nazareth, is the constant companion
of the pilgrim to Compostela, whether as Apostle, confessor,
witness, pilgrim or martyr, defender of the faith or warrior-
knight. His images are often accompanied by local references
relating to a particular time, and change accordingly: he hears
the prayers of the pilgrims depicted on the church doors of the
Hospital del Rey in Burgos, or he supports the king in prayer,
as in the altarpiece at Miraflores. In Germany and in other
countries, we find images of him protecting or crowning pilgrims. He is equally venerated as the patron saint of orphans,
and in eastern Europe as the patron saint of travellers. Finally,
at Wolfach in the Black Forest St James is venerated as the
saint who intercedes for a good death, the definitive journey.

In all the ways in which the Apostle is generally represented,
perhaps historical tradition often gives way to legend; there are
cultural and social, religious and political influences at work,
usually very much interconnected. Today it is sometimes hard
to recognize and understand them. The key to doing so is to
look to medieval humanity's faith in revelation, in the promise
of eternal life and the longing to be advancing towards it as
pilgrims.

Images of the figure of St James are like a mirror. In him
we see the longing of pilgrims of past times, and the deeply
felt desires of present-day pilgrims may also be reflected there.
This is true not only on the Way of St James in Spain but on
the many pilgrim roads in any country. In recent years many
thoroughfares and paths have been revitalized and definitively
waymarked so that there are currently many roads leading to
Santiago.

Lastly, an interesting observation: if the ways of depicting the Apostle have been many and varied, not less has been the diversity of popular names derived from his: Santiago, Iacob, Jacobus and Jakobus, Jacobo and Jakobo, Yago and Yacob, Iago, Tiago, Diago, Diego, Jacques, Jack, Jaime, James, Giacomo and Giacopo, Jaume, Köbesch – and so on.

Trust

The Milky Way lights holy fools
To one and many Santiagos
And the saint in many friendly guises
Helps his pilgrims to the shrine.

I met him, coming from Compostela,
And in thin enough disguise
– I knew him in our parting hug –
To show the way
To my own Santiago:
This perilous path
Through the canyons
Of the solitary heart,
Already undertaken
Though without a map
Or any inkling of its goal,
Suspecting that the end
Was in the beginning,
And lay always beyond –

For who shall reach
That final beach
Where the stars come down to the sea?

Howard Nelson

Part 13
Drawn by the Apostle
as by a Magnet

THE ROUTE

In Santiago

→ Santiago de Compostela: the name derives from one of two possibilities: *campus stellae* or 'field of stars' is the more popular, but *compostum*, 'burial place' is better accepted by scholars. The city of the Apostle is today the capital of Galicia. In the Middle Ages, together with Rome and Jerusalem, Santiago made up the trio of so-called 'great pilgrimages', and was then, as it is today, one of the largest centres of pilgrimage in the Christian world. Here the pilgrim reaches the longed-for destination and discovers that the *Camino* goes on: that life is a journey crowned with a goal, and that while life has many objectives it has only one goal; that our objective and our true goal is the way that leads to God, from whom we come and to whom we return. In short, the pilgrimage to the tomb of the Apostle is an image of life itself.

The cathedral is the central point of the city and is at the same time the reliquary of the Apostle St James. It is surrounded by various buildings that together form an architectural complex with the Romanesque church at the heart of it. The first church over the tomb of the Apostle was built by King Alfonso II 'el Casto' in around 830–40. The second, commonly known as 'la Basilica', was built by Alfonso III 'el Magno' on the same spot.

The cathedral, Santiago de Compostela.

It was destroyed by the Moorish commander Al-Mansur in 997. Bishop San Pedro Mezonzo (who is usually credited with the composition of the *Salve Regina*) rebuilt it in the year 1000. The construction of the existing church took place in three phases: from 1075 to 1088 under the direction of Maestro Bernardo, from 1100 to 1165 under Maestro Esteban, and 1165 to 1211 under Maestro Mateo. The building was consecrated on 3 April 1211. In style it conforms to the usual plan of a 'pilgrimage church' – that is, one that reinforces the idea of life as a pilgrimage by offering an ambulatory with radiating chapels so that pilgrims can perform a devotional circuit around the apse – the area where Mass is celebrated on the high altar and where relics are usually kept. The cathedral is rimmed by four *plazas* or squares: Obradoiro, Platerías, Quintana and Azabachería, also known as Inmaculada Concepción.

In the Plaza del Obradoiro, looking towards the cathedral's main facade, we have on our left the Hostal de los Reyes Católicos, instituted by the Catholic monarchs themselves to provide shelter for pilgrims. Work began on 2 November 1499, and to carry it out and administer the resulting foundation, the Archicofradía del Glorioso Apóstol Santiago was created. It still exists today, and has a worldwide membership dedicated to promoting devotion to St James and knowledge of the pilgrimage. On the right is the Colegio de San Jerónimo founded by Alonso III Fonseca, Archbishop of Santiago from 1507 to

1523, utilizing the fifteenth-century facade of the ancient hospital of the Azabachería; today it is occupied by the Rector of the University of Santiago and his administration. Behind us stands the Palacio Rajoy, built by another Archbishop of Santiago, Bartolomé Rajoy y Losada (1751–72). Today it is the ayuntamiento or town hall, and houses both the civic administration and some offices of the Xunta de Galicia or provincial government. The facade of the cathedral, whose baroque towers were erected over the Romanesque ones, is the work of Fernando Casas y Novoa, and was carried out between 1738 and 1750. The external staircase was built in 1606 at the behest of Archbishop Maximiliano of Austria.

A young Galician piper busks for pilgrims near the cathedral in Santiago.

The Plaza de las Platerías contains a splendid fountain featuring horses' heads, the Casa del Deán, seat of the Pilgrim Office, and the entrance to the Rúa Vilar. Pilgrims who can show their *credencial de peregrino* duly stamped, indicating that they have fulfilled the necessary distance on the *Camino* on foot, by bicycle or on horseback, will be awarded the *compostela*. In this square we find the only Romanesque portico of the cathedral opening on to the exterior, and on the left-hand doorjamb we find the date of its construction: 1103. Among the sculpture the figures of the prophet David (with his harp) and Adam at the moment of his creation stand out. In the lower part of the exterior wall of the cloister are the shops where silversmiths and makers of objects in *azabache*, or jet – typical of Santiago – carry on a thriving trade. In past times some of them made religious objects for the cathedral and for sale under licence from the cathedral chapter.

Passing into the Plaza de la Quintana we find the Torre del Reloj or Clock Tower, begun in 1306 and concluded in the baroque style by Domingo de Andrade in 1680. The square is on two levels: to the west is the Quintana de Vivos, while the lower one, sometimes called the Quintana de los Muertos, recalls the cemetery that once lay here and underneath the cathedral. In it we find the Pórtico Reál, entrance to the office of the Archicofradía del Glorioso Apóstol mentioned earlier, and the Puerta Santa or Holy Door, built in 1611, over which stand figures of St James and his two disciples, Theodosius and Athanasius; its side panels contain 24 figures from the stone choir-screen built by Master Mateo. This door is opened in Compostellan Holy Years, which take place in years when the feast of St James, 25 July, falls on a Sunday. Instituted in 1122 by Pope Calixtus II, the Holy Years were confirmed on 25 June 1179 by Pope Alexander III in a bull entitled *Regis Aeterni*. Because of irregularities in the calendar, corrected by leap years, Holy Years take place in a pattern, every 6–5–6–11 years.

On the other side of the square stands the monastery of San Pelayo or Paio. The Quintana de Vivos refers to the pilgrims who approached the cathedral by way of the Via Sacra, entering it through the Holy Door in Compostellan Holy Years. In the buildings located in the Quintana de Vivos giving on to the Via Sacra, pilgrims were invited to take off their old, travel-worn clothing and put on the garment of a pilgrim, with the phrase 'cast off the old man and put on the new', thus symbolizing the interior change taking place

Pilgrims' passports, stamped at every stage of the journey by churches, hotels and bars, are a wonderful souvenir.

in their souls. Later the old clothes were burned on a kind of pallet placed on the roof of the cathedral, before the ciborium, facing east. The spot is marked with a metal cross, and can be seen from the Azabachería or Inmaculada squares.

Leaving the Quintana and entering the Azabachería we skirt the Corticela, dating from the ninth century, though its existing fabric dates from the eleventh and twelfth centuries. Its purpose was to look after the tomb of the Apostle, but from ancient times it was a parish church for foreigners and pilgrims from which the interior of the cathedral could be reached through its doorway dedicated to the Reyes Magos or Three Kings.

The facade of the Azabachería, the north side of the cathedral, is neoclassical in style and was built by Ventura Rodríguez in 1757 to replace the earlier Romanesque one. In the Middle Ages this square housed the Paradise Door, which gave access to the Archbishop's residence and the monastery of San Martín Pinario. Moving down the slope we pass under the Arco del Obispo (Bishop's Arch), with the Palacio de Gelmírez on our left, and reach the Plaza del Obradoiro.

One of Galicia's many pipebands performs in the Plaza del Obradoiro in front of the Cathedral of Santiago de Compostela.

The existing cathedral, begun by Diego Peláez in 1075, is in the form of a Latin cross some 98 metres long and 67 metres wide, with interior arches more than 20 metres high (and in the lantern over the crossing, 32 metres). It has three naves and a triforium, divided by semi-pointed arches into ten bays. Inside, the Pórtico de la Gloria by Master Mateo, the lintels of which were installed on 1 April 1188, is outstanding amid the building's artistic treasures, but there are others: the chapel of the Cristo de Burgos; the crossing, whose easternmost columns incorporate statues of Zebedee and Mary Salomé, the parents of St James and St John; the Capilla Mayor or chancel, where a bust of St James holds pride of place (a staircase behind it permits pilgrims to give him the customary hug); the crypt, with the Roman mausoleum in which the mortal remains of St James were interred; these, together with the remains of his disciples Theodosius and Athanasius, are today kept in the silver reliquary on the altar. Within the east wall of the right arm of the underground crossing, archaeologists have found the burial vault of Bishop Theodomir, who died in 847 and who witnessed the discovery of the Apostle's remains.

Among the cathedral's features the Capilla del Salvador, behind the apse, merits special mention as the spot where work began on the present cathedral in 1075, in the reign of Alfonso VI. In this chapel during the Middle Ages the pilgrims received the certificate testifying to their arrival at the tomb of the Apostle. To the right is the Holy Door, which is only open

The swinging of the cathedral of Santiago's giant censer, or 'botafumeiro', is one of the sights the pilgrims long to experience when they reach their goal.

during Compostellan Holy Years. Other features include the Capilla de las Reliquias, the treasury, the museum with its many precious objects, the library, the chapter house and the cloister built by Gil de Hontañón and Juan de Alava in the sixteenth century.

Besides the cathedral, the city of Santiago houses many important monuments, such as the Palacio de Gelmírez, the monasteries of San Martín Pinario and San Pelayo de Antealtares, the convent of San Francisco, the Colegio Fonseca, Santo Domingo de Bonaval, the collegiate church of Santa María del Sar, the churches of Santa Susana and Santa María Salomé, the Museo de las Peregrinaciones, the Museo del Arte Moderno y Contemporaneo, and many more.

Stop and Think About It

'The longer you have been on the road, the better it feels to arrive' is an observation made by many pilgrims. They have seen, heard and experienced a great deal. Many things have made a strong impact. Some of these will keep echoing in the aftermath of the journey and will have to be resolved in hours of silence. None the less, the overwhelming emotion on arriving at Santiago de Compostela is joy.

The Arrival – Reality and Symbol

Our journey began with the Chinese proverb, 'The longest journey begins with a single step.' The initial feeling of desire and resolve is captured in Psalm 122 – a song of pilgrimage to Jerusalem – with the words, 'I was glad when they said unto me, Let us go into the house of the LORD.' The psalm continues in a way that all pilgrims to Compostela will recognize: 'Our feet shall stand within thy gates, O Jerusalem. Jerusalem is builded as a city that is compact together: Whither the tribes go up ... to give thanks unto the name of the LORD' (Ps. 122.1–4).

Standing in front of the cathedral in Santiago we may well be bereft of words. In the Pórtico de la Gloria a seated St James receives pilgrims at their journey's end, holding the *tau* or staff of redemption. He is at once reality and symbol.

The reality of arriving at the 'House of the Lord' should instil in us feelings of admiration, respect and gratitude. A longed-for goal has been achieved. For pilgrims of past ages too, Santiago was a symbol of the heavenly Jerusalem and, in addition, of the culmination of their lives and of union with God. Their arrival after months on the way of pilgrimage, their entry into the cathedral and, inside, the sight of the pilgrim people of God moving around the church – skirting the choir, passing around the ambulatory and the radiating chapels – until they reached the centre of the sanctuary, was a symbolic re-enactment of the words written by the visionary St John: 'he will dwell with them, and they shall be his people, and God himself shall be with them, and be their God' (Rev. 21.3).

Today the experience of arrival and of being drawn closer to St James, as if we are being pulled by the magnetic field generated by him here in his cathedral, continues to be of the deepest significance. It keeps undimmed the longing for 'the new Jerusalem', for the city of peace, the reign of justice over all the world and for a creation restored. This gives energy with which to look at life with fresh eyes and correct our course accordingly. It motivates us to set out again on the pilgrimage of life. Silence and prayer, recollected attention (for example, to the singing and liturgy going on in the cathedral) and meditation (perhaps on the figures and meaning of the Pórtico de la Gloria or some Gospel incident), are ways of expressing our hope for 'the new Jerusalem'. Whoever tries it will find God's encouragement in verse 8 of Psalm 32: 'I will instruct thee and teach thee in the way which thou shalt go: I will guide thee with mine eye.'

On Pilgrimage

I am walking to Santiago,
But that was then, and the bones of men,
Walled up, were walking still.
By the light of the great sun,
I watched them go,
And by rain-light and wolf-light, they pressed on,
As we were walking to Santiago.

And the mountains came and went,
With snow and bitter winds
And eagles but a touch away
Rocks where little birds ended their pilgrimage
In nets and the gasp of guns,
When we were walking to Santiago.

There were days of mud and cold and hunger
And uncertainty, when all hope was for shelter
And all that eyes could see
Was the horizon,
And all that ears could hear
Was the sound of footfalls,
As we were walking to Santiago.

Then there were days when nightingales sang,
And cuckoos called. There were rocks
Where small green lizards basked
And frogs sang in a foreign tongue.
And storks disdained us
From their apartments in abandoned belfries,
As we were walking to Santiago.

When we were walking to Santiago
I wondered why the rage of such multitudes
Left us only whispers as a guide.
The ghosts that clanked ahead
Were lost in darkness, where I had expected light.
Blind to their vision,
My feet fell always on the endless ground
As we were walking to Santiago.

One day I fell
When we were walking to Santiago.
Strangers helped me stand and then walk on.
A stranger in a shabby suit,
In some crowded city, seeing us lost, bone-tired,
Thinking us thirsty, gave cold water, all he had,
So we might walk on.
At a lonely place, a nun gave blessing, and embrace,
To hurry us along,
As we were walking to Santiago.

So we went, under the sun, over bleak places
Past bad dogs and storms of lightening
And red dust.
Past weariness, anxiety and sickness,
Past the kindness of strangers,
Beneath the eye of God,
Past the hospitality of grubby bars
And all the good wishes of an alien way;
Coming at last, on the fortieth day,
To Santiago.

Above the field of stars, the great cathedral
Leaned against the clouds.
Within the shadows there, were crowded
The bones of a dead man and
the singing of the quick.
And a stone that spoke to touching hands
And a jubilation that I could not touch,
And the vast silence of an elsewhere God
When we had walked to Santiago.

Later, we crept like mice
Back to that empty holy place
And brought to mind the face
Of the nun at the crossroads,
The man in the shabby suit
And the help of strangers' hands,
The busy barman bringing the gift of food,

And all these calling out along the way
To be remembered at Santiago.

That was years ago
And I
Am still walking to Santiago.

Doug Bayne

The 'Discovery' of the Apostle's Tomb in the Ninth Century

Historical documents relating to Compostela and dating from the ninth to the twelfth centuries place the 'discovery' of the Apostle's tomb in the early part of the ninth century, between 813 and 820. History and legend are intermingled in the account. The tomb was discovered by the hermit Pelayo in the vicinity of Mahía, and identified by Theodomir, Bishop of Iria Flavia, as the burial mound of the Apostle. The event was variously described as a 'discovery' and an 'invention', and the site as the holy grave of the Apostle where worship was rendered.

Modern historical investigation has revealed that well before the ninth century, both in the Iberian peninsula and outside it, there existed a firm belief that St James had preached in Spain and the western provinces of the Empire, and that after his beheading and martyrdom at the hands of Herod Agrippa in AD 44 (Acts 12.2) he was buried at or in *Arca Marmorica*, but whether this was a stone vessel or a place is uncertain. In the fourth century St Jerome recorded this tradition (in the *Breviarium Apostolorum*), as did the English Bishop Aldhelm of Malmesbury (650–709). St Isidore of Seville, in his *De ortu et obitum Patrum*, written in the middle of the seventh century, recorded that the Suevians and Visigoths identified Spain as the place where the holy Apostle had preached, and *Arca Marmorica* as the place of his burial. Despite the Muslim invasion of 711 and the destruction of the Visigothic kingdom, the new kingdom of Asturias and Galicia kept this jacobean tradition alive: the liturgical hymn, *O Dei Verbum*, written in about 785 and attributed to Beatus of Liébana, praises the

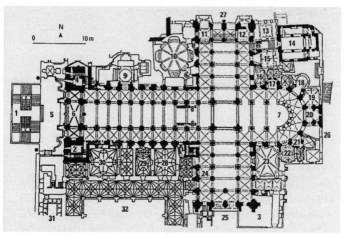

1 Crypt of the old cathedral/staircases
2 Tower
3 Clock tower
4 Tower
5 Obradoiro facade
6 Portico de la Gloria
7 Apse, High Altar and Crypt
8 Organ
9 Chapel of the Christ of Burgos
10 Chapel of the Blessed Sacrament
11 Chapel of St Catherine
12 Chapel of St Anthony
13 Chapel of St Andrew
14 the 'Corticela'
15 Chapel of the Holy Spirit
16 Chapel of the Immaculate Conception
17 Chapel of St Bartholomew
18 Chapel of St John

19 Chapel of St Peter
20 Chapel of the Saviour
21 Chapel of Our Lady of Azucena
22 Mondragón Chapel
23 Chapel of Our Lady 'of the Pillar'
24 Clavijo tympanum
25 Doorway leading to the 'Platerias' square
26 Holy Door
27 Doorway leading to the 'Azabacheria' square
28 Sacristy
29 Chapel of St Ferdinand
30 Chapel of Relics
31 Library and exhibition of capitals
32 Cloister
31 & 32 Cathedral Museum

Plan of the Cathedral of Santiago de Compostela

Apostle as the evangelizer and patron of Christian Spain.

To the basic tradition concerning the discovery of the tomb were added other narrative legends, brought together in the *Letter of Pope Leo*, a fifth- or sixth-century document attributed to a bishop or patriarch of Jerusalem. This was the first collection of Galician traditions concerning the Apostle, his disciples, his translation from Jerusalem to Iria Flavia and his burial *sub Arca Marmorica* in the 'western city' some 12 miles from Iria. Without naming the city, it refers to local features (such as Monte Ilicino, today the Pico Sacro); it also mentions the names of the disciples and the fact of their burial in the Apostle's mausoleum, and invites the reader to visit the same. Together with marvellous narratives, the *Letter* sought to gather up material and memories relating to early Christianity in Spain and in Galicia. Alongside this source of hagiography we may place the foundation of a church at Meilan by Odoario, Bishop of Lugo, in the seventh century. It was dedicated to St James – indicating that in this instance, at least, the ancient jacobean tradition was taken for granted.

The grave of the Apostle was found in dense woodland. The burial chamber was a small room decorated with marbles and had a floor paved with mosaic, below which were interred the saint's remains. Alongside lay the bodies of the disciples, whose tombs survive. The grave formed part of a more complex Roman building: a pagan mausoleum with a *cella* or sanctuary that was taken over by Christians in the earliest phase of evangelization. Archaeological excavations revealed that the mausoleum was situated in a Roman and Visigothic necropolis, in use from the first to seventh centuries.

It is important to be aware of the 'discovery' and the reasons for identifying it with the tomb of St James on the part of those who found it. On the face of it they must have felt they had clear proof, including the testimony of viable authorities. Today, the conclusions regarding the authenticity of the tomb of the Apostle, based on archaeological investigation, can also be said to offer an effective defence.

BETWEEN PAST AND PRESENT

The Pórtico de la Gloria – Welcome and Invitation

The main portico of the cathedral of Santiago de Compostela, sculpted by Master Mateo in the late twelfth century (and since 1750 protected from environmental pollution by the facade set in front of it), receives the pilgrim as if into the vestibule of heaven, and invites him or her to enter. It recalls the vision of St John:

> behold, a door was opened in heaven: and the first voice which I heard . . . said, Come up . . . and I will shew thee things which must be hereafter . . . and, behold, a throne was set in heaven, and one sat on the throne. And he that sat was to look upon like a jasper . . . and there was a rainbow round about the throne, in sight like unto an emerald. And round about the throne were four and twenty seats: and upon the seats I saw four and twenty elders sitting . . . and in the midst of the throne, and round about the throne, were four beasts. (Rev. 4.1–6)

To this doorway, with its symbolic wealth of figures and its whole orientation centred on the figure of Christ, we should come with something of the attitude of the pilgrims of centuries past, even though those who admire it today are equally impressed by the expressive figures and the artistry. We can obtain a general view of it with the aid of the diagram on p. 169, but the detail must be left to individual scrutiny of the monument itself.

Pilgrims approached the end of their journey dirty and exhausted, some singled out by sickness, but filled with joy and hope. In the lower part of the central column, a little above the monsters, they were faced with their own image: humankind, debased by sin and enveloped in the dread of hell but also hoping for pardon and redemption. From the depths of this image there bursts forth the Tree of Life, from the wood of which, according to legend, was wrought the cross of Christ. It is often called the Tree of Jesse, since his genealogical line, depicted as a tree, was destined to be crowned by the Messiah.

The pilgrim's gaze passes from the root of the Tree of Jesse upward to the seated and serene figure of St James, who receives the pilgrim in the name of the Lord. Like the *tau* held by the saint, the pilgrim's staff here becomes a symbol of the cross and of redemption, a sign of the completion of his pilgrimage. St James, having entered into the glory of God once

St James welcomes his pilgrims: Portíco de la Gloria, cathedral of Santiago de Compostela.

his earthly life was over, now accompanies pilgrims as they enter the house of Christ, who is seated above on a throne as judge of the world. He shows the five wounds of his passion and proclaims: 'I am acquainted with the sufferings of life on earth. I am a righteous and merciful judge.'

Apart from the figure of Christ, which stands out above all else, the other figures of the Pórtico also command attention. They acquire their interpretation in relationship with Christ and from Christ, whether it is in the columns of the lower left, which show the serious figure of Moses carrying the stone tablets of the Law, of which Christ was the fulfilment; or the smiling Daniel whose faith was so strong that no danger could shake it (or so his scroll attests); or Isaiah, whose finger indicates the future and announces Emmanuel, 'God with us' (Isa. 7.14). Even Jeremiah, who does not wish to open his scroll – 'behold, I cannot speak: for I am a child' (Jer. 1.6) – and wanted to run away to avoid having

The figures of Isaiah and Moses in the Portíco de la Gloria.

to announce Israel's misfortunes, prefigures Christ, the bearer of Good News. Or in the columns on the right, where the Apostles stand as heralds of the message of Christ; and here the two 'Sons of Thunder' (James and John) are deep in conversation – perhaps about the differences between their means of announcing it. John prefers the word and the book; James, the road and the staff of the pilgrim. To the left stand the figures of the Old Testament, mainly prophets; to the right, those of the New Testament. All of them are inclined towards the crown of the Tree of Life: Christ in the centre, and surrounding him the four Evangelists, represented as persons with their respective attributes; the eight angels holding the instruments of the Passion; and all of these are framed, in a semi-circular arch, by the 24 'ancients' with their musical instruments, modelled on those of the medieval troubadours. They represent divine quietude and praise. They and all the other figures invite pilgrims to enter into the glory of the Lord, praising him and giving him thanks.

Part 14
Open Like a Scallop-Shell

THE ROUTE

From Santiago to Finisterre

➡ Cabo Fisterra/Cape Finisterre: a lighthouse at the end of a great pier of granite jutting out into the Atlantic Ocean marks the westernmost point of Spain and of the European continent. Before the discovery of the Americas it was believed to be the end of the world. As was natural, there was no lack of legends and stories, such as that of the city of Duxo, sunk in the sea; just as there were many modes of devotion to the pagan gods, such as the cult of the sun. Such tales and traditions piqued the curiosity of medieval pilgrims and led them to make their way to the fabled spot to see the sunset. For them, the setting sun was less a symbol of death or finality than of the never-ending cycle of regression, of conversion (from an old life to a new one) and, thus, of Christ, who conquered darkness and brought new life.

➡ It is said in Galicia that God, having completed the work of creation in six days, rested his hands upon the earth and left the marks of his fingers as the marvellous *rías gallegas*, or fjords. And God was captivated by the beauty of this combination of land and sea, and was pleased.

➡ Corcubión: this pretty town has given its name to the *ría*.

➡ Carnota: this town is famous for its *hórreo*, or elevated granite store-chamber for maize and grain, said to be the largest in Galicia.

➜ Muros: this is a picturesque spot on the *ría* with a small church dedicated to the Virgin of the *Camino*.

➜ Noya/Noia: note the fortified church of San Martín with its impressive west door. In the cemetery of the church of Santa María a Nova there are tombstones marked with the signs of the medieval craft-guilds. All along the route covered so far the *cruceiros*, or wayside crosses, merit special mention.

➜ Padrón: this is a town characterized since antiquity for its port and for the extraction of minerals from its nearby mines. The Phoenicians traded in this area, as did the Romans around Iria Flavia. It is traditionally said to be the site where the body of St James came to land, brought by his disciples from Palestine. The wayside crosses along the coast and the small islands of the Ría de Arousa mark the stages where it rested on the way. Beneath the altar of the church of Santiago one can see the *pedrón* or large stone that gives its name to the locality. It would seem that this is either a stone altar or a marker stone indicating the commencement of the *Via Antonia*. It is popularly and piously believed that the stone boat in which the mortal remains of St James were transported was tied to it on coming ashore – as the text below the altar indicates.

STOP AND THINK ABOUT IT

Repeatedly on the Way of St James one encounters the *pecten maximus*, the scallop-shell. Here on the sea-coast around Finisterre, Padrón and other places, pilgrims habitually collected the semicircular bivalve shell, characterized by two small lateral flanges and fourteen radiating ribs, and would take them home as visible proof of having reached their destination. Thus over time the shell changed from being the symbol of pilgrims in general to one typical of the pilgrim to Santiago.

The symbolism of the scallop-shell can be interpreted in many ways and is found in many religions. Very early on Christians saw it as a symbol of the begetting of the Son of

God of the Virgin Mary. The pearl (Christ) is formed of the mutual self-giving of heaven and earth. Jesus' parable (Matt. 13.45) relates how a wealthy man sold all he had to possess an especially beautiful pearl.

The Scallop-Shell – Emblem of the Pilgrimage

For pilgrims to Santiago the scallop-shell had at the same time practical functions and symbolic meaning.

- Pilgrims used the shell as a serving vessel for food and drink.
- It was also visible proof of having completed the pilgrimage.
- Attached to clothing, it served as a safe conduct. It was considered a grave crime to rob a pilgrim.

The scallop-shell, emblem of the pilgrimage to the tomb of the Apostle St James the Great.

Its ancient meaning and view of it as a sign of the union of the heavenly and the earthly is once again restated. Compostela became a meeting place of the divine and the human at the farthest point of the known world (as it was then), at the limit between the finite (Cape Finisterre) and the infinite. The scallop-shell symbolizes the pilgrim's encounter with the celestial.

Living the Meaning of the Scallop-Shell

The scallop-shell is the outward sign of being a traveller on the Way of St James. It is also a symbol of all those experiences and encounters that come together on the Way: of all that in each one of us begins to grow, and of all that has begun to shine again and to give forth light.

Camino Tale – The Parting Gift

At some point this company must part
and once more pursue paths solely set
our time together though will remain
woven into a rich memory cloak we share . . .
the warp our lives shared side by side
the weft our perusals in pilgrim path places
the colours richly steeped in autumn kindnesses
the pattern, divinely sprinkled with joy,
sparkling moments of earth beauty intensity.
The laughter and happiness carried
both hearts and bodies along the miles,
with an eye kept fondly on one another
so that all would journey safely on.

Colin Hudson

BETWEEN PAST AND PRESENT

St James – History, Legend and Faith

Regarding St James the Great and the disciple of Jesus of Nazareth, very little has come down to us in historical terms. On the other hand, from the fifth century onwards – and above all from the discovery of his tomb sometime between 813 and 820 – there are numerous accounts concerning the finding of the tomb, the person and the actions of St James, the legendary happenings and miracles relating to him, emanating from pilgrims, confraternities, military orders and so on.

Today a veritable galaxy of legends surrounds the figure of St James and the pilgrimage route, of which the essential ones are found in the *Golden Legend* of Jacopo de Voraigne and from then on – according to one's degree of interest – in the various guidebooks. They will not be repeated here; rather we will concentrate on the few existing references about the historical and biblical figure of St James, about the importance of the legends and the results of both for the faith of the pilgrim.

The Historical and Biblical St James

James, brother of John and son of Zebedee, was among the first disciples whom Jesus commanded to follow him (Matt. 4.20; Mark 1.19). Together with his brother and Peter he belonged to the 'inner circle' of disciples, and he is frequently named in the Gospels as one who accompanied Jesus at important moments – for example, the raising of Jairus' daughter (Mark 5.37), on Mount Tabor (Mark 9.2), on the Mount of Olives (Mark 14.33) and other occasions. He and his brother received from Jesus the name *Boanerges* or 'Sons of Thunder' (Mark 3.17).

In general in the biblical accounts we always find St James in the company of his brother. All the events refer to both sons of Zebedee together. Later, in the Acts of the Apostles, he clearly goes on to be the first of the disciples to bear witness to his risen Lord on suffering a martyr's death. He was beheaded by order of King Herod Agrippa I in AD 44 (Acts 12.2).

History and Legend (a 'Garland' of Legends)

The activities of the Apostle in Spain following Christ's ascension are legendary – and, going by the New Testament, improbable. It would seem that St James enjoyed little success and returned to Judea. The belief that he spent time in Spain derives from a comment of St Jerome's in the fourth century, assigning to the Apostles for their respective missions certain areas of the world as it was then known. The elder 'Son of Thunder' was allocated Spain, where he evangelized and was buried. This is what Beatus of Liébana asserts in his *Commentary on the Apocalypse*. Thus even at this early date there is a reference to the tomb of the Apostle in Spain, although he was beheaded in Jerusalem and the tomb in Spain was found much later. The Visigoths also venerated St James. His evangelization of Spain and burial there were already accepted as fact in the sixth century. King Recaredo (who later converted from Arianism to the Christian faith) referred to him as 'the sole patron of Spain' as early as AD 587, and the third Council of Toledo (AD 589) stipulated that everyone protect pilgrims to Santiago.

An important testimony comes from St Isidore of Seville in his work *De orta et obitu patrum*, written early in the seventh century. Here it is said that James, son of Zebedee and brother of John, evangelized the western parts of Spain and sent the light of his preaching to the very ends of the world; that he died, beheaded by the sword on the orders of the tetrarch Herod; and that he was buried in the place known as *Arca Marmorica*. The text mixes biblical tradition, history and legend. It also mentions the legend, known since the fifth century, of the miraculous conversion of the magician Hermogenes, whose disciples Philemon and Josias prompted the beheading of the Apostle. To this was added a 'garland' of legends about St James. One of them describes the Apostle's tomb in similar terms to those used by St Isidore. The sequence of legends can be arranged and characterized as follows:

- legends involving the saint's activities: the two already mentioned, and that of the saint's death;
- legends surrounding the translation of his body (the boat, the wild bulls, Queen Lupa, the monastery of Sinai, Granada, Mérida);
- legends about the discovery of the tomb;
- legends in which the saint appears as a secondary personage (the dream of Charlemagne; the battle of Clavijo (as *Matamoros*);
- legends relating to the pilgrimage (the miracle of Santo Domingo de la Calzada; the pilgrim saved from the devil).

We today often have problems with legends – but is there ever a legend without a grain of historical truth?

The Witness of Faith in Images

The legends have not come into being without reason. Often they have been transmitted verbally, shortened or elaborated according to the situation of the narrator, and have evolved into almost incredible stories. Is there an element of truth behind each of them? It may be hard to believe this. Legends are not primarily concerned with historical facts, yet historical relationships may none the less be described in them. Legends primarily transmit images in which human faith is clarified and strengthened.

We must learn to view and interpret this varied 'garland' of legends about St James and the pilgrimage route from the medieval standpoint and in a medieval context. In this understanding of life and the world, a person who had been a witness to the Son of God made man was highly esteemed and regarded. To venerate him, entrust oneself to his keeping, pray to him and follow him as a pilgrim was a deeply felt desire. In addition, these actions helped to build up and inspire the pilgrimage as well as the struggle against human evil, both personal and social. Some legends about St James, perhaps arising in this way, were useful in promoting political interests; an example of this might be the so-called 'dream of Charlemagne'.

The historian Claudio Sánchez Albornoz has called attention to the fundamental interest of such legends. He points out that the belief that the body of Christ's disciple was buried in Santiago had powerful consequences for the history of Europe. The supposed finding of the body of St James was very likely used to rally the seemingly hopeless resistance of a handful of Asturian mountain tribes to the enormous power and domination of Al-Andalus. The finding of the tomb of the Apostle was, for the threatened warriors of the north of Spain, like a promise of divine aid on the side of their arduous struggle, year after year, against the Islamic forces.

A historical and critical perspective is only part of the story. However, as with all legends this one contained a kernel of mythic truth that ensured that it came to have more influence than any strictly historical account. In legends, facts and dates are incidental, and the concept of 'truth' takes on another meaning. The legend – that is to say, the version that has to be read – expresses in words and images what human beings of faith, in their personal experience and firm trust, perceive and wish to convey. Legend is human history as it has been lived, which has an influence upon the future. It moves some to action and allows others to bear up under adversity; still others find in it the spark of hope that banishes defeatism and prompts a fresh beginning.

Part 15
Life Can Only be Lived Facing Forwards

Returning Home from the *Camino de Santiago*

Today we are going to change our customary practice of being on the Way or on a journey. We have to organize our return home according to our schedule and the means available. We have to make our farewells: Santiago has been the goal and continues to be the partial end of our journey or our state of being on the road of life. With luck we will have time for a farewell journey to the cathedral.

'The pilgrim journey leads to our own front door.' It reminds us that 'Whoever takes to the road also travels homeward.' Today this refrain becomes a reality. We are on our way home, having completed our pilgrimage to Santiago de Compostela. Some pilgrims are perhaps now recalling their departure, while others are thinking, happily or not, about the daily round they will soon recommence. Modern travel makes possible a rapid return home. For the pilgrims of past ages – restored both externally and internally by their stay in Santiago – the return journey was a task of equal magnitude to that of reaching the Apostle's shrine in the first place. For modern pilgrims the return is easier, but to arrive home well in body and soul is important, the culmination of a life-changing and life-affirming journey. As a means of achieving this, let us review the daily experiences of our pilgrimage under four headings, phrased as questions, and then bring them together as a prayer.

The Danish philosopher Søren Kierkegaard expressed the view that 'life can only be lived forwards, but understood only by looking back'.

Let's reflect on the second part of the quotation:

1 What meetings, experiences, knowledge and images of the journey do I retain?
2 What inward understanding and outer manifestations of it do I bring to those around me?
3 What has changed in me as a consequence of being 'on the way'?
4 What do I have to allow to grow and mature in myself?

The first part of the quote can best be approached through a brief consideration:

On the *Camino*

I went to Santiago de Compostela,
Seeking myself and God.
Changed, I return home
Rich in experiences
Outer and inner
I return to my old life
To places where
I re-encounter the familiar,
Where I work and rest,
Where I wanted to keep on living.

The perplexities, the problems and the people
Continue to be the same.
Only I am not altogether the same,
As the person who one day set off.

I see it all in a new way,
Free of coercion.
Delving deep in the familiar
I am on the road of life.

Now I don't *have* to
Love, work, suffer – I am able to . . .!
Living has become a gift
Because I live from inside, from God.

Oh God!
To live anew can only be done facing ahead
Along the pilgrim road of my life
With your blessing.

Source unknown

Consideration in retrospect of the pilgrim journey reveals its similarities to the journey through life, and – especially from the perspective of mature years – results in a satisfying sense of integration, wholeness and direction towards the life that lies ahead.

Parallels: Reflections of a Pilgrim Returned

Yes, I will, yes – to herself or to him,
And as a journey of a thousand miles
Starts with a single step, so any life
Begins, no turning back, for her, or for
That pulsing fragment of a guiding star.
About the way must, and about must go,
Weaving through Spring's shining flowers, and snow,
Dark woods and chasms – push, push,
Teeth grit and the sweat flow – Roncesvalles,
Valcarlos – reborn at the abbey Mass,
Baptized again in God's sweet rain, where wind
And spirit moves. March on, swing with me, lass,
In the strength of our youth, by the broad fields
And trout streams, 'til the faces and fields yield
To the traffic of life, and the spring of our back
Twists and sets to the many things,
Many things stuffed in our pack.

Still the way takes us, meanders and winds
Through the city's roar, and the sharp slopes taking your
    breath.

Life's losses, stubbed toes, hard knocks leave their mark –
And so we learn to lean. Learn in our third age
Companionship. Across the meseta's long, level land
Learn to value most the soil and the birdsong.
No hues of fashion but the coloured earth,
No music but the skylark's song,
From village fountain take our water-wine.
Lumpen trivia of the world's wants put aside,
Packs lighter, lift our eyes to the star's guide.
March on, march on! Hear, on the other side
Of that blue mountain range the great sea's roar!

Howard W. Hilton

The *Camino de Santiago* – a European Itinerary

From Don Elias Valiña, the parish priest of O Cebreiro, who died in 1989, has come down to us the view that 'the Way of St James and its ancillary routes formed throughout Europe a gigantic vertebral column by which the whole of Europe was unified and invigorated'. The functions of the vertebral column are well known: it unifies, supports, holds together, provides balance, enables movement, protects the necessary and vital nervous system, and allows its owner to walk upright.

The Way of St James, including its local contexts and its network of secondary routes, developed all these functions between the end of the ninth century and the time of the French Revolution. From very early on it was a thoroughfare along which culture was carried and transmitted, on which pilgrims from all the European states were to be found, mutually aiding and protecting one another, living their faith in the act of taking the human road with God the creator of the world and Christ the judge of the universe, and trusting in St James, the first Apostle that gave his life for Christ. Freed from the weight of their guilt and sins they set out for their homelands, some settling in other territories and some remaining in Spain.

As early as the *Historia Compostelana*, written between 1109

181

and 1140 in Santiago, the European dimension of this road or pilgrimage route was clear; the ambassador of the Moorish emir Al Ben Yusuf (1106–42), on his journey to Compostela, expressed his admiration in terms that can be summarized as 'Who is this, so great and so important, to whom Christians without number from both sides of the Pyrenees render homage and before whom they pray?' and he observed that 'the multitude of those coming and going from Compostela barely leaves space free on the road westward'. People replied that this was St James, the Apostle of the Lord, whose body was buried within the confines of Galicia and whom France, England, the Italian states and those of Germany and all the provinces of Christendom venerated. Above all he was venerated in Spain, as her patron and protector.

This 'traffic jam' on the Way of St James, caused by throngs of pilgrims from all over Europe, gave rise to its profound influence in European history. The pilgrimage to Santiago de Compostela was an essential contribution to the growth of a shared European consciousness. Within this were four main strands:

1 The fundamental religious and Christian sense and practice of the pilgrimage.
2 The variety of artistic and cultural expressions and the cross-fertilization of styles.
3 Political and economic interests and the interplay between them, and the legal framework and practical measures that arose to protect pilgrims.
4 The fund of experiences between individuals and the social interactions between groups that created mutual interdependence and solidarity on the *Camino*.

Along the whole length of the Way of St James today's pilgrim and traveller can find multiple examples of these four strands of influence (although for brevity's sake this book has made reference to only a few). The *Camino de Santiago*, forged by pilgrims and pickpockets, saints and sinners, artists and courtiers, scholars and clerics, knights and craftsmen from all over Europe, and endowed with a network of roads and their offshoots, became a European cultural thoroughfare, linking Spain with lands and peoples at the farthest reaches of the continent.

The pilgrimage was not free of contradictions – ever. The lack of propriety among those on pilgrimage led Thomas à Kempis to record in his *Imitation of Christ* that those who often go on pilgrimage seldom became more holy through their experience. On the larger scale of events the *Camino* was subject to conflicts of every kind, to epidemics and local outbreaks of violence, including those caused by heresies and schisms. In short, from the Lutheran Reformation of the sixteenth century onwards, the various religious and political conflicts, national interests and continual wars in Europe implied serious reversals for the *Camino*. It was repeatedly attacked and arose again to offer its many services to pilgrims at the same time as it fearlessly presented its message and image of life in the light of the figure of the pilgrim Apostle. The hardest and most acutely felt blow to this European dimension of the pilgrim route was attributable to the French Revolution, to the wars and sequestrations of property in various countries (for example, in Germany in 1802 and Spain in 1835), which led to the suppression of the monasteries, guesthouses and hospitals that had contributed so enormously to the network of European routes. With this were destroyed the access roads, and the concession and control of pilgrim safe-conducts passed into the hands of state officials. Meanwhile, in the nineteenth century, even if in fewer numbers, pilgrims continued to travel to the tomb of the Apostle, just as in the Iberian peninsula the pilgrimage survived on a reduced scale. The forced cessation of the activity of many charitable institutions and the suppression of the monasteries and convents along the *Camino* meant that fewer pilgrims came. The rediscovery of the remains of the Apostle in 1879 (hidden in 1589 for fear of Sir Francis Drake) and the Holy Year 1895 went some small way to reviving the pilgrimage, though it had never really died out. In 1937, in the middle of the Spanish Civil War, the Apostle was again proclaimed patron of Spain. The excavations beneath the cathedral in 1948 brought to light interesting discoveries. In reality it was the new interest of the international historical research community and its conferences and exhibitions that played a major part in the revitalization of the ancient idea of pilgrimage. From then on, in the various countries and regions there began to arise associations, societies and confraternities of St James, and the old pilgrim halts began to revive, as in San Juan de Ortega and O Cebreiro; guidebooks for pilgrims on foot and on organized study tours and pilgrimages began to appear. Pope John Paul II met with the young people from all over the world in Compostela in 1989 on the occasion of World Youth Day. Europe was once again to be found, using all the modern forms of travel as well as the ancient mode of walking, on the *Camino de Santiago* and in the city of Compostela.

With all the problems implied by the union of religion and mass tourism, the essential character of the *Camino de Santiago*, in its guise of 'European Cultural Itinerary' (as it was declared by the Council of Europe in 1987) or 'Patrimony of Humanity' (a title awarded it by UNESCO in 1993), is an important contribution to the development of a European consciousness.

May the faith that moved pilgrims throughout history and which was a bond among them in the same sense – above and beyond all national differences – also impel us in our day ... to become pilgrims in constructing a society that is founded on tolerance and respect for human beings, on freedom and on the awareness of common bonds.

(from the Council of Europe's *Declaration*, mentioned above, 23 October 1987)

In order for that to happen it will be necessary to delve again into the Christian roots of the *Camino de Santiago* and draw from them strength for a spirituality of the pilgrimage routes that is fitting for our times, whether as a pilgrim on foot or other mode of transport, or as a mechanized traveller. This is also a contribution to a united Europe, to a Europe with diverse nations that have created their individual cultures but that are parts of a whole to which pertain certain common civic, cultural and historical experiences. One such experience is Christianity, and particularly the pilgrimage road to Compostela: as Goethe put it, 'Europe was born of the pilgrimage, and Christianity is its mother tongue.'

To Pilgrims

Go,
From your birth
You are on the way.

Go,
An encounter awaits you.
Who with?
Perhaps with yourself.

Go,
Your steps will be your words,
The road, your song,
Your weariness your prayer,
Your silence at last will speak.

Go,
With the rest,
But come out of yourself;
You, who see yourself hedged round by enemies,
You will find happiness.

Go,
Although your spirit does not know
Where your feet are taking your heart.

Go,
Another comes to meet you
Seeking you,
So that you can find Him.
At the sanctuary at the end of the road,
In the sanctuary in the depth of your heart,

He is your peace,
He is your joy.

Go,
It is the Lord
Who goes with you.

*Angel Fernández de Aránguiz SCA (translated by
Laurie Dennett)*

Acknowledgements and Sources of Illustrations and Photographs

Illustrations and photographs on pages 8, 17, 26, 67, 78, 88, 89, 103, 116, 125, 138, 147, 155, 168 and 172 are used by permission of Peter Müller, author of the German edition, *Wer aufbricht, kommt auch heim* © 2009 Verlag am Eschbach der Schwabenverlag AG.

Photos on pages 14, 18, 30, 32, 82, 109, 110, 111, 112, 126, 128, 131, 132, 141, 142, 156, 157, 158 and 159 are used by permission of the Confraternity of St James, 27 Blackfriars Road, London SE1 8NY, UK.

Acknowledgements and Sources of Poetry

Unless otherwise indicated, all poems are taken from the Confraternity of Saint James Bulletin. Every attempt has been made to obtain the permission of their authors. In most cases this was granted, but in a few it proved impossible to locate the authors concerned.

'A Message to Pilgrims', anonymous, from a wall in the Monastery of Lluc, Majorca, translated by Janet Richardson.

'An anonymous poem on a wall outside Nájera', translated by Laurie Dennett.

'He is Your Peace', anonymous, carried by a South African pilgrim and presented at Refugio Gaucelmo.

Julián Barrio Barrio, 'Route of brotherhood', in *Peregrinar en espiritu y en verdad*, pastoral letter for the Compostellan Holy Year, 1999, translated by Laurie Dennett.

Andrew Connolly, 'Night thoughts (O Cebreiro, October 2000)'.

Doug Bayne, 'On Pilgrimage'.

Neil Curry, 'Checks and Balances'.

John Davidson, 'Crossroads'.

Gerardo Diego, 'The Cypress of Silos', in *Versos Humanos* (Human Verses), 1925, translated by Laurie Dennett.

St Ethelberg's Centre for Reconciliation and Peace, 'A Prayer for an End to Violence'.

Angel Fernández de Aránguiz SCA, 'To Pilgrims', translated by Laurie Dennett.

Minnie Louise Haskins, 'The Gate of the Year'.

Howard W. Hilton, 'Parallels: Reflections of a Pilgrim Returned'.

Colin Hudson, 'Camino Tale – The Parting Gift', 'The Star Over the Field'.

Jane Morton, 'Pilgrim's Map'.

'My Friend', anonymous, on a wall in the Abbey Church of Conquest, translated by Laurie Dennett.

Howard Nelson, 'Leaving', 'Trust', in *Trust and Tears: Poems of Pilgrimage*, London, Howard Nelson, 1998.

Piers Nicholson, 'The Camino'.

Karin Temple, 'Claustro', 'El Camino', 'Matamoros', 'Puentes (bridges), in *Peregrina*, Spokane, 2003.

Index of Places

Listed are only places on the Spanish part of the pilgrim's way, from the Pyrenees to Cape Finisterre.